CLASSIC KITS

Collins

ARTHUR WARD
CLASSIC KITS
COLLECTING THE GREATEST MODEL KITS IN THE WORLD
FROM AIRFIX TO TAMIYA

DEDICATION

For Eleanor and Alice. Study this book carefully. It features part of your inheritance – you lucky girls!

First published in 2004 by Collins, an imprint of HarperCollinsPublishers 77-85 Fulham Palace Road Hammersmith London W6 8JB

Collins is a registered trademark of HarperCollinsPublishers Ltd.

everything clicks at www.collins.co.uk

10	09	08	07	06	05	04
7	6	5	4	3	2	1

Copyright © 2004, Arthur Ward

A catalogue record for this book is available from the British Library

ISBN 0-00-717695-3

Designed by Christine Wood

Printed and bound by Printing Express Ltd, Hong Kong.

contents

Daddy Progs reading his book.
Saturday January 10th 2004

by Eleanor 1/2

**Illustration of author by
Eleanor Ward. Age 7½**

An apology

This book is not a list of every kit made by each kit manufacturer. There is simply not the space to do so and, frankly, I lack the ability and desire to do it. Many of today's companies simply re-package kits which originated elsewhere; keeping track of everything is almost impossible. The commercial marketplace features a great deal of 'mould sharing' whereby old kits are re-badged and re-boxed by value-added resellers in the manner common in the IT industry. Consequently it is very difficult to keep track of the provenance of mould tools which may have originated in England years ago — especially those made by FROG — or even with kits which originated more recently in Japan or Korea. Apart from a few exceptions most of the brands shown in this book originated some time ago.

There are many worthy checklists in print. Probably the best available is published by John Burns of America's 'Kit Collector's Clearinghouse'. I admire the ability of men such as John — although I have no idea where they find the energy required to compile such directories — but my interest is simply to try and capture some of the 'essence' of what plastic modelling means and has represented to generations of enthusiasts. I want to engender a feeling of warm nostalgia — the memory of happy days building plastic kits, encouraging recollections of relaxed and innocent times when, apart from the odd occasions when one lost a tiny but essential part deep into engulfing carpet pile, making kits was fun.

Introduction

By the late Victorian age, industrialisation and the increased shift from rural to urban dwelling compelled massive lifestyle changes amongst Britain's population.

The coming of the 20th Century hastened this revolution. Individuals – mostly men – went from their homes to a separate place of work and came back at a regular hour each day to enjoy a certain amount of free time. Time at ease could be spent in pursuit of sport, in the pub or club or, of course, at home in the fulfilment of a personal interest. The hobbyist was born.

During this period of social and economic reform, the aforementioned industrialisation also delivered mass production, enabling the manufacture of a vast range of components, previously the province of skilled artisans. So now, along with Ford Model 'T's, an assortment of much smaller machined gears, cranks and con rods rolled out of factories everywhere. With the availability of standardised miniature components, the scale model enthusiast was born.

As the title of this book suggests, the focus of the narrative is a survey of the most famous and enduring kit brands. Other than Bill Bosworth's late lamented Accurate Miniatures from the 1990s or Freddie Leung's Hong

¼th scale Spitfire Mk1a the first of the 'Superkits' (1970)

Dinky Builder, 1950's.

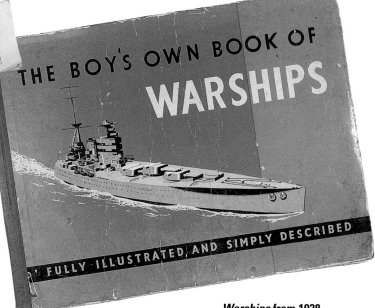

Warships from 1938.

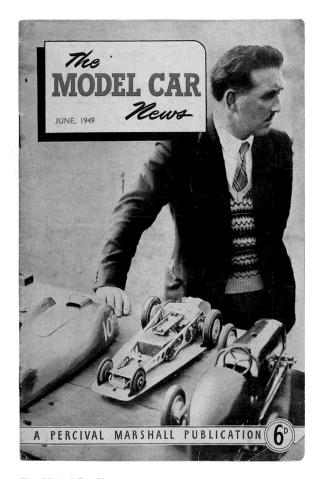

The Model Car News,
1949.

1972 Tamiya kit
catalogue.

Kong-based Dragon Models, founded in 1987, the brands featured herein are either long gone, or have been with us for decades.

Space prevents mention of many of the recent additions to the plastic kit firmament, whose introduction tends to contradict those 'wise counsels' who claimed the day of the polystyrene construction kit had passed. So, to all those newcomers: a big well done and please forgive the omission of your products in a survey of 'classic' kits. Who knows, one day in the future an enthusiast like me will write a book concentrating on all those firms from Eastern Europe such as Zvesda, AML, Eduard, Mirage Hobby, ICM, Lotnia and Roden; the newer Chinese manufacturers, most notably Trumpeter; Canada's Modelcraft; North America's MRC; Korean brand leaders Academy as well as Japanese new kids on the block like AFV Club and Tasca.

Neither is this book the place for stories about vacuum-form kit manufacturers such as Airmodel, Aeroform, Formaplane and Rareplanes or those firms who produce resin models. Of the latter the biggest and best is certainly VLS, established by master modellers Francois Verlinden and Bob Letterman in the 1980s. I well remember

Mr Verlinden's superb dioramas gracing the pages of *Military Modelling Magazine* in the 1970s. Accurate Miniatures, Cromwell Models, CMK (Czechmasters), Resicast and others, are creditable manufacturers in this field.

Dating from April 1962 this edition of the ever popular *Hobbies Weekly* was the usual collection of "Up-to-the-minute ideas, practical designs and pleasing and profitable things to make." Subjects ranged from making model miniatures to building full size divans!

The Model Engineer,
July 1950.

1. History and Development of Scale Models

***Thrilling Stories* – full of the sort of ripping yarns which captivated pre-war aero enthusiasts.**

Since time immemorial man has made miniature replicas of his world. The ancient Egyptians placed tiny models of the kind of worldly possessions the deceased would find indispensable in the afterlife (one 11th dynasty prince was entombed with an entire miniature imperial guard for protection). Tiny clay models of war chariots, dating back to 2800 BC, have been discovered at the site of the ancient Sumerian city of Ur and some 5,000 years later the Romans are known to have mass-produced cast lead 'flat' miniature soldiers – possibly the first commercially available scale models. Many cultures made similar offerings to the gods in an effort to thank them for the annual harvest or, with rather less benevolence, for victory in battle against an enemy.

Indeed, it was the increasing sophistication in warfare that proved the real stimulus to scale models, as we know them today. As England, Spain, Italy, France and the Netherlands – Europe's principal maritime trading nations – expanded their overseas dominions, the huge burden of policing trade routes was placed upon their navies. Expanding dramatically, their fleets devoured acres and acres of oak woodland as merchant vessels and fighting ships were built to protect the new territories.

Mass production of these rival armadas required shipwrights to be sure they could manufacture ship after ship to the same pattern in a consistent and accurate manner. In the days before computers and calculators, when many skilled craftsmen were illiterate and, anyway, incapable of reading complex plans, the best method of explaining the complexities of design and

***Marvellous Models*, Puffin, 1940s.**

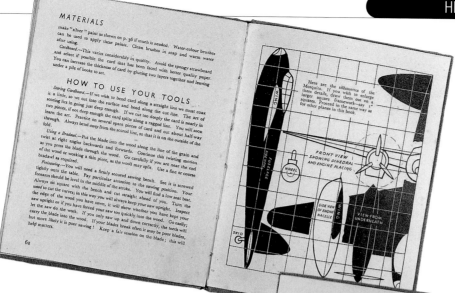

describing precisely how components fitted together, was to build an accurately reduced-scale replica of the intended vessel.

The fabulous Admiralty models prepared in England and those created in the support of competing maritime powers, were the first truly accurate scale models produced. Their construction required the development of techniques of modelling and finishing familiar today and encouraged the introduction of many tools and materials still in use. Many of these fine models survive in museums today.

Being largely landlocked and surrounded by potential enemies, it comes as little surprise to learn that Bismarck's newly unified Germany focused more on martial prowess. Consequently Bavaria, notably, became the centre of a burgeoning model soldier industry first manufacturing flats and later producing solid metal figures from famous manufacturers such as Heyde and Llegeyer. Similarly, Napoleonic France placed great emphasis on the achievements of its land forces and shortly after the demise of Bonaparte's First Empire, the French firms of Lucotte and, later the more famous Parisian firm of Mignot, established a pattern of scale model soldiers which survives to this day.

Together with items of cast and extruded metal, and long before the advent of polystyrene, Edwardian toy and model manufacturers experimented with a whole range of man-made plastics. These were mostly derivatives of nitro cellulose materials. In 1870 the Hyatt brothers invented 'Celluloid' in the United States as a suitable material for billiard balls. Shortly afterwards, in 1872, the Smith & Lock company patented the very first

Spreads from Richard Chick's *First Book of Model Aircraft*, 1944.

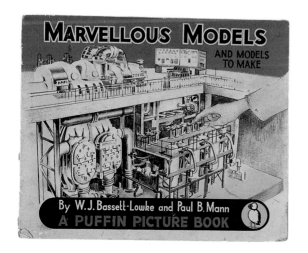

War shortages dictated a more modest treatment for Bassett-Lowke's Economy Catalogue.

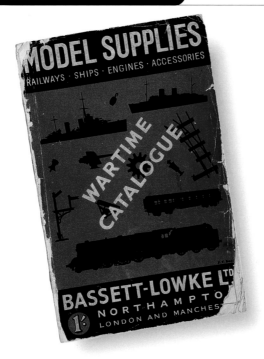

1950s English-made ½th scale 'Do It Yourself' bedroom suite.

Dinky Builder, **1950's.**

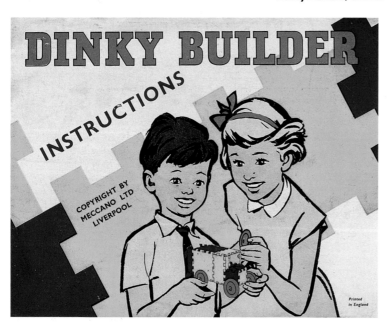

injection-moulding machine in an attempt to hasten the manufacture of such items. Unfortunately the new plastic proved unsuitable for the new process and Smith & Lock's revolutionary new machine would have to wait until some new raw material was synthesised.

Germany, rapidly becoming a major player in the chemical and dyestuffs arena, also had a fledgling toy industry. This had a facility with tin-plate and, using a spin-off of the burgeoning canning industry, quickly learnt how to print designs on this thin metal. German toy makers also turned to new methods in synthetic and composite production that were a by-product of their chemical industry.

In 1919, German scientists had at last produced a thermally stable cellulose plastic – cellulose acetate. A revised injection-moulding process was invented – the most famous system being that patented by the American Leo Baekeland, inventor of the famous phenol-formaldehyde resin/plastic 'Bakelite'. Although, today's polystyrene injection moulding machines are far more sophisticated, their principal mechanisms would not be unfamiliar to the early American and German pioneers of such technology.

Early 20th-century German production seriously challenged established British manufacturers like William Britain, who was then largely employing traditional hollow casting techniques using lead or an assortment of equally malleable alloys. Interestingly, just as Britain and Germany were vying for economic and military supremacy, their rival toy industries were fighting their own battles for dominance in the field of 'war toys' with each producing a profusion of soldiers, artillery and 'dreadnought' battleships!

During that time there were not really any model kits of the type we take for granted today. However, young and old were adept at assembling scale model locomotives and the myriad buildings required to complete a train layout (W. Britain's 54mm lead toy soldiers were originally designed to people toy railway layouts). An early example of the kind of business partnerships taken for granted in the modern kit industry occurred in

1900 at the Paris Exhibition when British model locomotive manufacturer Wenman Bassett-Lowke met Stefan Bing, the German owner of expensive top-quality toys and trains. Thus began an enduring relationship, which resulted in the production of some classic model locos and culminated in the Trix range of construction sets in the 1960s.

Prior to the Second World War the majority of scale model construction required a fair degree of craftsmanship and an understanding of basic metal or wood working techniques. Even the fuselages of early aircraft miniatures came partly formed from a solid block of wood and needed considerable working before they remotely looked like the illustration on the box lid.

Some manufacturers, however, embraced the new synthetics. They soon provided easier-to-assemble scale replicas, taking the labour out of the hobby and paving the way for the modern toy and hobby industry.

Principal amongst these was the brand Bayko, which utilised the revolutionary properties of Bakelite to make an assortment of miniature building blocks and James Hay Stevens' Skybirds.

Skybirds, a range of wood and mixed-media model aircraft, are justly famous for establishing the scale of ½nd – or 6ft to 1 inch. FROG, another British manufacturer, who had branched out from rubber-powered flying scale models to a new range of static display models, Penguins, immediately adopted this scale. FROG's Penguins were manufactured from cellulose acetate butyrate, but because of the material's fugitive nature, few examples survive today. More about Skybird and FROG later.

Embracing a range of traditional and modern construction skills, the growing scale models hobby evolved to generate a thriving support industry of publications, tools, adhesives and paints. However, although principally aimed at schoolboys, the name of London's annual Model

A partly shaped wooden 'Skycraft' kit from the 1950s, typical of models available before polystyrene took hold.

Before Hamleys there was Gamages – 1961 Model Book.

Wartime catalogue of a popular exhibition revealing German aviation developments – well, it was one use for all those wrecked enemy airframes!

Engineering Exhibition reveals the rather purist nature of the hobby at this time.

The Second World War proved the real catalyst for the growth of the modern kit industry which millions of us take for granted today. The loss of traditional sources of raw materials – notably rubber as the Japanese conquered British colonies in the Far East – forced the further exploration of techniques for synthetic production and plastic moulding. Developments in electronics, especially in aviation where numerous moulded components were required, created an enormous demand for plastics manufacture. Ironically, the discovery and capture of German manufacturing plant at the war's end turned out to be a further encouragement.

Even more starved of raw materials than Britain, Nazi Germany was forced to accelerate the development of the manufacture of plastics. With a tradition of inventiveness and having perfected some leading-edge production processes, the Third Reich was also in the van of injection moulding.

As the conscripted allied armies advanced on the shattered country, many over-curious former engineers took advantage of the opportunities presented by so much abandoned plant. Rather unscrupulously perhaps, details of German innovation and, allegedly complete injection-moulding machines, found their way back to Britain and America, forming the basis of both nations' post-war plastics industry.

The Second World War was a catalyst for the modern kit industry in another way, too. The rapid developments in military technology, especially in aviation – the modern jet engine came of age during the 1939–1945 conflict – provided a huge range of new subjects for kit manufacturers. Dozens of blockbuster war films, books and magazines provided all the raw material required to stimulate fertile young imaginations. Also stories of real-life heroes like Audie Murphy, Douglas Bader and Adolph Galland encouraged the demand for specific representations of vehicles and fighter planes. Further accelerated by the cold war and the space race, which each spawned dozens of new inventions, the post-war kit industry developed into a boom time for manufacturers worldwide.

As mentioned previously, the earliest construction kits of the type we take for granted today were manufactured by the British firm of Skybirds which was founded by James Hay Stevens, a well-known aviation writer and illustrator of the 1930s and 1940s. Stevens' replicas certainly established the internationally standard ½nd scale and the Skybirds range numbered more than 20 models by 1935. However, they were not really plastic kits, being constructed from mixed media, with wood, acetate and metal components.

Being highly unstable and inconsistent, the first commercially available plastics were unsuitable for the earliest injection-moulding machines.

The Micromodels range of card models extended to ships, trains and historic buildings.

Interior Details of War Planes **from 1942. Notice the fighter's Ring-Sight, a long-obsolete instrument. RAF reflector sights were still a state secret.**

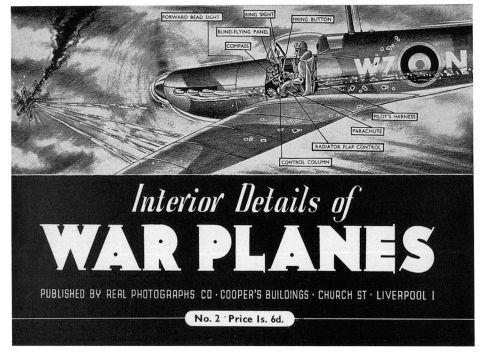

Although the most famous surviving early plastic is Bakelite, an American invention, the credit for production of the first true plastic construction kit, made entirely from a synthetic cellulose acetate, must go to Britain.

In 1932, two brothers, Charles and John Wilmot, founded International Model Aircraft Ltd (IMA). IMA produced a range of rubber band-powered flying model aircraft under the brand name F.R.O.G. (**F**lies **R**ight **O**ff the **G**round). Each model aircraft, constructed from a combination of pressed pre-painted tin with delicately formed pre-stressed paper wings, could be trimmed to perform countless feats of scale acrobatics. Indeed at the time, 'FROG' competitions were very popular. Youngsters vied for superiority as they held their fully wound models on the ground and watched them accelerate and climb skyward as the rubber unwound and the propeller began to spin. Peter, a friend of mine who remembers flying such models, told me that enthusiasts generally replaced the supplied dowel rod, against which the elastic 'motor' was tensioned inside the fuselage, for a substitute of greater diameter. Apparently, the thinner material often broke if the rubber was over-taut, causing enormous torque which

In the early-1970s, pen maker Platignum produced a range of card models in an attempt to revive the craze of pre-war years.

Flying Review, January 1961.

Aero Modeller Annual, 1961-2. On the cover is 'P11.27' – the 'Harrier' prototype.

U.S. Army Aircraft published in 1942. Written and illustrated by aircraft enthusiast Roy Cross. Twenty-five years later he would be painting similar machines on Airfix box tops.

collapsed the lightweight fuselage.

Although they were essentially toys, FROG aircraft, especially their high-speed 'Interceptor' monoplane, were an immediate success and IMA prospered. In 1936 it introduced a range of accurate ½nd scale model aircraft. IMA had decided to exploit the growing 'air-mindedness' which prevailed amongst men and young boys whilst the growing diplomatic tensions in Europe encouraged an arms race with numerous new aircraft designs abounding.

Delightfully evocative and eminently collectable 'Skybirds' packaging for their pre-war ½nd scale Hawker Hurricane multi-media kit.

Scale-line Constructional Plan of 'Albemarle Glider Tug', ½nd scale, 1942.

Being non-flying the new range of IMA aircraft were branded 'Penguins'. The first three Penguins were accurate scale replicas of some of Britain's contemporary (but, compared with the designs emanating from Hitler's Germany, still woefully inadequate) front-line aircraft – the Hawker 'Fury', Gloster 'Gladiator' and Blackburn 'Shark'.

As mentioned above, being constructed from somewhat unstable cellulose acetate, the various parts of FROG Penguin kits were often subject to twisting and

warping in the box prior to assembly by the purchaser's eager hands. Apparently, the main reason for this inconsistency was caused by IMA's practice of paying piecework wages to its moulding-machine operators. These early machines were hand-operated and the acetate material feeding needed time to cool sufficiently before it was released from the mould tool. Not surprisingly, operators, concerned with increasing their take-home pay, frequently failed to pause the process sufficiently for things to cool down. Consequently, parts sprang from the mould with an inherent 'memory', which led to warping. IMA were aware of this problem and did their

Veron 'SAAB J.29', typical of the solid wooden kits of the 1950s.

level best to prevent it, even resorting to cementing together larger pieces, such as fuselage halves, and packing them, suitably braced, into the kit boxes. Celluloid was also used for the smaller transparent canopy parts. Whilst not prone to as much distortion as the larger pieces, these had a tendency to yellow after a short time.

Despite shortages, IMA continued producing their Penguin range throughout wartime and had added replica ships, racing cars and modern saloons to the range.

Finding a better plastic material more suitable to the new science of injection moulding became a priority.

Change, however, was in the air. The exigencies of total war encouraged the manufacture of myriad items from synthetic materials including control switches, goggles and oxygen masks, pistol grips and transparent map overlays. The scarcity of sources of natural raw materials further accelerated technological development. By the war's end, techniques of injection-moulding polyvinyl chloride (PVC), and the rigid and stable plastic polystyrene, were finally perfected. PVC was a material that dated back to the mid-19th century,

Hobbies Weekly,
May 1948.

Hobbies Weekly,
July 1946.

**Aeromodels ¼th
Scale 'Comper Swift',
1940.**

The Adventure Annual adding robots and spaceships to the lexicon of 1950s youth.

'Sky Devils Air Circus' – a typical entertainment for Britain's air-mad aircraft buffs.

but which had traditionally been laboriously slow-cured in single moulds. Actually, it was only after suitable plasticisers had been added to PVC in the 1930s that this new material became useful at all.

As developers tried various formulas, one of them, America's Du Pont, launched the world's first polyamide – better known as Nylon. Among other things, Nylon was essential to the mass-production of reliable military parachutes. The previous silk ones, made from a material minutely studied by Du Pont chemist Wallace Carothers to point the way to his new synthetic, had a tendency towards static causing the silk parachute to fail and 'corkscrew'.

In Britain two major developments were of equal value in wartime. ICI's Alkali Division synthesised polyethylene, a material essential to the production of radar. Later, the same company developed polymethyl methacrylate, or 'Perspex', a material whose shatterproof qualities made it perfect for aircraft canopies.

Polystyrene as such was first discovered by the German apothecary Simon in 1839 but it was not until another German, Staudinger, had more carefully studied its molecular structure that its true potential was realised. As late as 1937 ICI were involved in standardising an economical method of stabilising polystyrene during storage – essential if the limitations exhibited by acetate were to be avoided.

By the early 1940s most of the uncertainties of injection-moulding polystyrene had been overcome and this

Lincoln International 'Bristol Britannia', 1963.

method became the principal way of forming thermo-plastic materials.

Basically, injection moulding works like this: plastic material (usually in granulated form) is put into a hopper, which feeds the heated injection unit. The plastic is pushed through a heating unit by a recip-rocating screw and is softened to a fluid state. At the end of this unit a nozzle directs the fluid poly-styrene into a cold mould. Clamps hold the mould halves (or multi-sections) securely together. As soon as the plastic cools to a solid state the mould opens automatically and a series of ejec-tor pins push the moulded pieces attached to a frame or 'runner' (usually incorrectly called the 'sprue') out on to an automated production line. Here they are bagged, which is espe-cially important for transparent parts to prevent scratches, and boxed. Incidentally poor design of ejector pin location some-times leaves raised unsightly disks on visible parts of the model, requiring lots of tedious work to remove them.

With polystyrene the perfect raw material and injec-tion thermo-moulding the ideal process to shape its temporarily pliable form, the scene was at last set for the revolution in the toy and hobby industry which reverberates to this day.

Modern Wonder, 1938.

All-electric Erector set, 1940s, invented in 1913 by American manufacturer Gilbert. Very similar to Frank Hornby's Meccano, Gibert's Erector quickly became the dominant brand in the US and actually forced Meccano to close its fledgling factory situated in New Jersey. Incidentally, in 1990 the independent French Meccano bought the US Erector trademark and began marketing sets branded Erector Meccano in North America!

2. Going the Distance – the Classic Brands

Original artwork for the WWII 'Classic Fighters' set that Airfix packaged exclusively for British retailer Marks & Spencer in the late 1970s.

As with other products, differing brand names of kit manufacturers appear and disappear. However, due to the massive initial financial outlay required to enter the kit-manufacturing business in the first place, generally only those firms prepared to wait some time for a profitable return on investment – those in for the long haul – decide to enter the fray in the first place.

Fortunately, some of today's names would be familiar to modellers of many years ago. It's with these famous brands, principally Airfix, Revell-Monogram, Tamiya, Hasegawa, Italeri, ESCI, Bandai and Heller, that we shall begin. However, before we do, it would be unreasonable and alphabetically incorrect not to mention Accurate Miniatures in a book titled *Classic Kits*!

ACCURATE MINIATURES

I first became aware of the name Bill Bosworth whilst leafing through US publisher Schiffer's excellent tome, *The Master Scratchbuilder*. There, in the company of other modelling heroes such as Alan Clark and John Alcorn, a photograph of the genial founder of America's Accurate Miniatures depicted him proudly displaying his beautiful scratch-built Japanese WWII Mitsubishi 'G4M' 'Betty' which Bill built to an enormous ⅟₃₂nd scale with a wingspan of 31 inches.

Shortly after seeing Bill's talents for myself and learning all about his fastidious attention to detail, I purchased one of Accurate Miniature's earlier kits, an excellent ⅟₄₈th scale replica of a personal favourite, Grumman's barrel-chested 'TBM Avenger' torpedo dive bomber. Like all other Accurate Miniature kits, the attention to detail and finesse of the parts in the thoughtfully packed box were remarkable and to my mind have never really been bettered.

I was fortunate to actually meet Bill during the IPMS Nationals in Telford in 1999. I was attending because my commemorative history of Airfix was being simultaneously launched on Dave Hatheral's Aviation Bookshop stand and on Humbrol/Airfix's stand. We shared the train journey back from Shropshire to London before parting company and heading for home – Bill had further to go – he lives in North Carolina, USA. We discovered we had a lot in common; a love for models and both our professional careers began in the advertising industry.

In their short life (Accurate Miniatures were incorporated in 1993 and ceased production in 2001), the company released models of more than 20 different types of aircraft, fixed wing and helicopters, and they produced numerous variants of many of their chosen subjects.

Each kit displayed the uncompromising attention to detail and accuracy that had previously characterised Bill's scratch building and had quickly established Accurate Miniatures as being quite different from the norm.

One of Accurate Miniatures' last kits, which I'm sure is going to be destined to become a modern classic, is their substantial ⅟₄₈th scale 'B-25B Mitchell'. This aircraft was immortalised when it mounted the audacious long-distance raid on the Japanese mainland shortly after Pearl Harbor. This version and its standard Army Air Force counterpart (Doolittle's raiders were stripped of all non-essential weight to enable them to complete their one-way journey) serve as a fitting testament to Bill's efforts.

In his *Plastic Aircraft Kits of the Twentieth Century (and Beyond)*, 'Guru of glue' John Burns says that following its demise, some Accurate Miniatures moulds were sold to Italeri. Apparently a new company entitled Accurate Hobby Kits might rise phoenix-like from the ashes. Let's hope so.

Accurate Miniatures' superb 'TBM-3 Avenger'.

AIRFIX

Where it all began, the 1949 'Ferguson Tractor'.

Fittingly perhaps, Airfix, the subject of my last book and a lifelong passion, is almost at the head of the list of enduring giants (if its position hadn't been usurped by Bill Bosworth's Accurate Miniatures it would have been precisely where Mr Kove, who founded the company in 1939, would have wanted). Kove came up with the name 'Airfix' – suggesting 'Fixed with Air' – so that his firm would appear at the front of trade directories. He founded the company in 1939 but it entered the model kit business in 1949.

As the original definition of the name suggests (many still believe it is derived from 'fixing' aircraft), Airfix originally made air-filled toys and novelties. These were mostly made of rubber, a commodity that became increasingly scarce following Japan's military conquest of British plantations in the Far East, forcing the firm to adopt synthetics.

Struggling to keep in business, Airfix was often forced to use myriad acetate scrap bits and pieces and even strip the insulation coatings off unwanted electrical flex in order to feed its hungry moulding machines. Fortunately, by producing acetate lighters and at one point actually cornering the home market for moulded plastic combs, Airfix survived the war years and the immediate period of austerity that followed. However, almost by accident, the firm took the first step on the construction-kit ladder.

Having acquired some injection-moulding machines – the latest in high technology – Airfix was commissioned by British tractor manufacturer, Ferguson, to produce a number of ready-assembled scale replicas of their newest tractor for use as a sales promotion piece. When Nicholas Kove, a wily opportunist adept at profiting from circumstance, was invited to provide a further quantity of these miniatures, boxed as unassembled pieces, he asked Ferguson if he could offer them for retail sale. Not surprisingly the tractor manufacturer jumped at the chance for such free 'PR'.

Airfix Toy Catalogue, early-1960s.

Unlike all Airfix kits that followed, the Ferguson tractor was moulded in acetate, which was a difficult material to work with and subject to distortion, encouraging frequent customer returns. Nevertheless, the tractor sold very well.

Encouraged by energetic young executive Ralph Ehrmann, who had brokered the deal with Woolworth and later rose to become Chairman of the entire Airfix group, Kove agreed to further pursue kit production by branching out into the production of new and different replicas. What seemed like an initial setback when Woolworth demanded a better wholesale price forced Airfix to abandon the use of boxes as packaging and supply unassembled pieces in simple plastic bags attached to paper headers; this proved a successful expedient. The classic Airfix plastic kit in its polythene bag was born!

The adoption of clear plastic bags meant that customers could see the contents of each kit without opening the package and risking either damaging or losing the tiny parts. A combination of Ehrmann's astute commercial activities, and the shrewd buying practices of the late John Gray, pointed the way to a future in kit production. Gray began his career at Airfix as a buyer

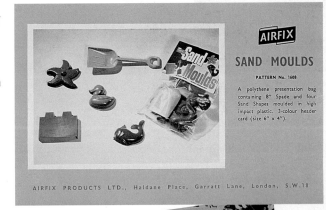

Examples of the toy range. Notice the charming innocence of juxtaposing the Tea Set and the Sand Moulds with the F. N. Rifle.

The Airfix F.N. Rifle in all its glory!

and profited from an extended supplier base and the dramatic reduction in the cost of polystyrene – a far better material than acetate as a substance from which to mould kits aimed at youngsters.

Airfix's first 'own brand' construction kit proper was the release of a tiny miniature of Francis Drake's *Golden Hind* in 1952. Moulded in polystyrene 'DS' – a new formulation that included a rubber component and was ideal for kit manufacture – the *Golden Hind* far exceeded sales forecasts.

Kove was reluctant to move away from a winning formula and thought Airfix should simply continue with model sailing ships. However, although the tiny 'Classic Ships' range was to grow and include numerous other vessels including *HMS Victory*, *The Great Western* and the *Santa Maria*, Ehrmann encouraged the firm's diversification. Soon a replica *Spitfire* was added to the range – almost an inevitability in post-war Britain – and the first in a long line of such aircraft, considered 'bankers' by most model manufacturers.

However, 1953's 'Spitfire BTK' was of doubtful authenticity and provenance, bearing a curious similarity to American firm Aurora's larger quarter-scale 'Spitfire' – even down to the erroneous decals! The 'new' 'Spitfire' was so bad that it encouraged a young modeller called John Edwards to write to Airfix suggesting that he could do better.

Hopefully, readers will allow me to spend a little time recounting details of John's short life (he died in 1970 aged only 38) which came to light following the publication of my last history of Airfix. His brother Peter told me about John's life before Airfix and it read like a thriller – I was only sorry that I hadn't been able to include it in the earlier book. Every Airfix veteran has told me that John was a charming, talented and very engaging chap but what I discovered reads more like a novel by John Le Carré or Len Deighton than anything to do with the gentle hobby of plastic modelling.

According to Peter, after John left school at Braintree, "graduating with 'flying colours' and passing matriculation with credits without even bothering with homework", he joined his uncle's photography business in Bayeux, Normandy. Although he "slogged away" in his uncle's darkroom for months, learning the tricks of the photographer's trade and perfecting his French to boot, he later nevertheless decided to return to Braintree. There he joined the Crittall Metal Window Company as a 'Window Design Draughtsman' and learnt the finer points of engineering draughtsmanship.

However, the story of precisely what John did when National Service beckoned immediately afterwards is even more enlightening and especially relevant to his later employment at Airfix.

Following his experiences in

Original 'Albatros DV', 1957.

1960s Press Advertisement

France, John had demonstrated a particular facility with languages. He was as comfortable with German as French. Posted into the Royal Artillery he found gun laying somewhat boring and his new-found proficiency as a linguist little used.

John was asked if he could cope with learning another language – Russian. He said he thought it would be straightforward (his brother told me that John soaked up knowledge "like a sponge") and with his usual aplomb mastered the language in weeks. He was posted to the Intelligence Corps (I Corps) and soon found himself garrisoned behind the Iron Curtain in Berlin, a city then divided equally between the Soviet, American, French and British occupying powers.

John's first job with I Corps was to monitor Russian radio traffic. After a while he was involved with the interrogation of 'cross overs', those emigrants from East Berlin who sought asylum in the west – the Berlin Wall was yet to be built. Peter Edwards told me that John's role at this time was to try to help build a complete dossier of Soviet strength in personnel and equipment. Eventually, John and his colleagues noticed that a squad of Soviet conscript soldiers were quartered close by and, tasked with manning a mobile rocket-launcher kept secured in a commandeered barn, were in the habit of abandoning their charge and nipping into the local town for a bit of rest and recuperation.

The opportunity to study this hitherto secret Russian weapon proved too much of a lure. When they were sure the Russian soldiers had left, John and his colleagues began their covert reconnaissance and broke into the Soviet arsenal hidden within the barn to record every detail of the armaments they found.

Being a keen modeller, it simply wasn't enough for John to photograph, measure and analyse every detail of the Russian missile system – he prepared plans and decided to build a scale replica of what he saw. Stealthily, he sneaked back to the British sector to begin planning this.

John then commenced scratch building a model of the new multi-barrelled rocket launcher. "Which was appreciated by all and sundry," said Peter. "I think he got his sergeant's tapes for that one," he laughed.

Now, with "the bit between his teeth", John proceeded to secretly build a collection of models of *all* the Soviet equipment in the Berlin theatre. His clandestine museum was exhibited on a trailer as a part of a travelling road-show which toured each quarter of the allied

½th scale Lifeguard Trumpeter, 1959.

Airfix/Bachmann Mini Planes.

First edition 'OO and HO' 'Farmstock'.

command, all this activity under the Soviet's nose whilst the Cold War was at its height.

Offered a commission to officer rank if he stayed in the army, John, by now married, declined and decided to return to 'civvy street'. Whilst back at Crittalls, in his spare time he built the first of the then brand new 2/- Airfix aircraft kits – the venerable 'Spitfire BTK' which was first available in 1953. Not surprisingly, Airfix's early and distinctly dodgy 'Spitfire' didn't much impress John Edwards. However, another kit purchase, a 1/72nd scale 'B25 Mitchell', by new US manufacturer Monogram, was a revelation.

Determined that British kits could be as good as those made in America, John answered an Airfix press-ad offering the position of design draughtsman. To boost his chances during the interview, John not only took references and details of all his qualifications and experience, he brought suggestions for the improvement of Airfix's fledgling 'Spitfire'. Armed with his own technical drawings, an improved version of the Airfix 'Spitfire' he had built himself and an example of Monogram's ground-breaking 'Mitchell', "which he revealed with a flourish, if I know my brother" said Peter, he warned the South London firm not to be too complacent.

"This is what you will soon be up against,"

he cautioned. As the interview drew to a close "the Airfix people went into a huddle," recalled Peter. Quickly they asked John when he could join. Without hesitation John told them he could start the next morning! The rest, as Airfix tyros will know, is history and as Peter said proudly: "The good old die was cast!"

Two years following the release of 'BTK', Airfix released a version of Johnny Johnson's 'MKIX Spitfire' ('JEJ'). Designed by John Edwards, this much-improved version of Mitchell's famous fighter was enhanced and retooled in 1960. Fittingly, this fine replica remained in the Airfix range for nearly 50 years and is a tribute to Edwards' skill.

Following his death, magazines heaped praise upon John Edwards. *Aircraft Illustrated* wrote: "John had been at Airfix for 15 years, almost from the beginning of the company, and was personally responsible for directing the design of all Airfix construction kits. It is only necessary to compare the early Airfix kits with such models as the Boeing 'B-29', 'HP O/400', 'He 177', 'Bulldog' or 'Sea King' to see what vast improvements were made. John's latest venture was the introduction of the new range of 1/24th scale kits, but he has sadly only lived long enough to see the first, the magnificent 'Spitfire' I, put on to the market."

Perhaps May 1971's *Airfix Magazine* obituary says it all: "Mr Edwards leaves a fine memorial in the big range of kits he has designed and which continue to give pleasure to millions of modellers throughout the world."

First edition Airfix catalogue, 1962.

Veteran 1/72nd scale Messerschmitt Bf109G-6 (1965)

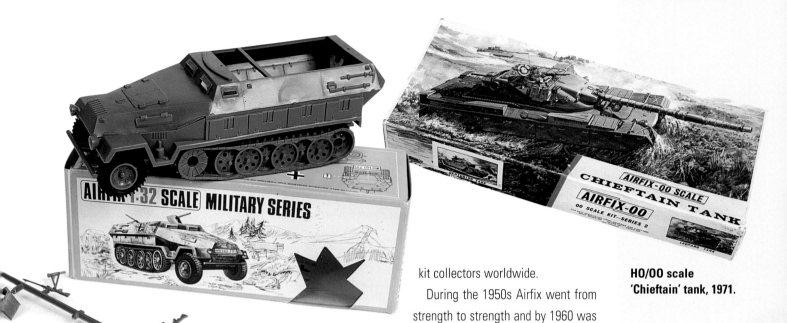

½nd scale ready-made German half track.

HO/OO scale 'Chieftain' tank, 1971.

kit collectors worldwide.

During the 1950s Airfix went from strength to strength and by 1960 was a big enough brand to warrant its own monthly consumer magazine. The inaugural edition of *Airfix Magazine* appeared in June of that year and was so successful it was to survive on and off until 1993. In 1962 Airfix published its first kit catalogue, the beginning of a tradition that has continued into the 21st Century, and now numbers more than 40 editions.

One of the secrets to Airfix success is the fact that it has employed so many gifted artists and illustrators to create its famous box art. Beginning with Charles Oates, Airfix went on to commission the talents of great artists like Roy Cross, a successful aviation artist who worked exclusively for Airfix for about ten years from late 1963. Still painting, for the last 30 years Roy has built an enviable reputation as a prominent marine artist. I was lucky

It is generally accepted that John's involvement with Airfix raised the bar in kit design, introducing innovations such as movable control surfaces and internal detail. Not surprisingly his criticisms of the appropriately short-lived 'Spitfire BTK' (recently re-released in bagged format on its 50th anniversary but using the mould of Airfix's seminal 'Mk1a' from the late seventies, the original tool having been revised to produce the first edition of Johnny Johnson's 'MkIX') means that original examples are 'rarer than hens teeth' and sought after by

A pocket money purchase dating from 1959, the year of the author's birth, Airfix's delightfully simple ½nd scale Hawker Typhoon.

Allegedly one of the rarest Airfix kits –
'Avro 504K', limited edition produced for
Quantas Airways' Golden Jubilee, 1970.

Definitely rare – *SS France* from
1963. The mould no longer exists.

Trio of 1/32nd scale old timers,
1962–1964.

enough to be introduced to Roy Cross whilst I was writing my last book about Airfix. I concentrated on his career in that book and touched on his time at Airfix in *Celebration of Flight*, his illustrated biography that I co-authored and which focuses on his aviation art. Roy's story is well documented and this isn't the place to repeat it. Other 'Airfix artists' include the chap who introduced the airbrush to Airfix box art in a big way.

However, readers might like to learn more about another famous Airfix artist, Brian Knight, who like Pete Edwards above, contacted me following the publication of my history of Airfix.

Like Roy Cross, Brian is one of the artists who add value to Airfix packaging with the addition of their wonderfully evocative illustrations. Equally, Brian also paints as actively today.

Brian was born in Reading in 1926 but is as bright and enthusiastic as a man half his age. Roy Cross, two years Brian's senior, also seems to defy the years – maybe there is a secret ingredient in Gouache paint which beauticians have overlooked!

Like many a youngster of his generation, Brian aspired to becoming an airman and hoped one day to join the RAF. He made model aircraft but although he enjoyed Penguins and Skybirds kits (when he could afford them) his favourite pursuit was scratch-building. Apparently, he used to fashion replicas from hard woods – his favourite was Sycamore because of its close grain.

"I have been drawing since the age of about four or five," Brian told me. "I guess most kids start then, but I was able to develop it more." As the Second World War

'Sheriff of Nottingham' Figures.

'Wild West' Playset, 1960s.

Airfix box top rough for
Lockheed 'P-38J
Lightning'.

Airfix box top rough for
HMS Hotspur (1964).

Airfix box top rough
for ½nd scale
Grumman 'Widgeon'.

Airfix pencil rough for
HMS Cossack box.

Pretty exciting promotional photograph of the Airfix 'Sherwood Castle' Playset. One can understand why, in the 1960s, the company relied on artists' skills to fire young imaginations.

Roy Cross artwork for 'Sherwood Castle Set'.

'Sunderland III' in Roy Cross box artwork.

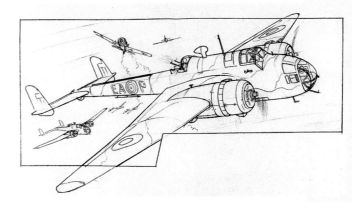

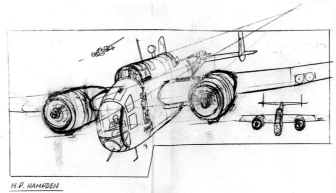

H.P. HAMPDEN

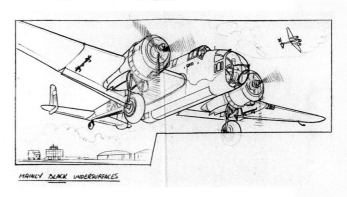

MAINLY BLACK UNDERSURFACES

Box top roughs by maestro Roy Cross for 1968's 1/72nd 'Hampden'.

dawned and "the idea of doing anything artistic became out of the question", Brian joined Miles Aircraft as an apprentice draughtsman. He soon graduated into their design section. An early project Brian drafted was Miles's 'M52' supersonic aircraft. After this he joined an agricultural manufacturer and designed combine harvesters and associated agricultural machinery. Such subject matter hardly inspired Brian and very soon he moved on again.

His next move was to join the fledgling Atomic Energy Authority at Harwell. They had recently established a brand new studio and soon Brian rose to the position of studio manager there. "We did what politicians couldn't do for themselves," he told me. "They knew that the tax-payer was paying out all this money towards atomic energy research and that the only way it could be explained was by clear diagrams. So, I now became a technical illustrator – no longer a draughtsman." Employed at Harwell between 1947 and 1957, Brian developed a valuable facility for accurately describing the features and mechanisms of complex systems and structures. An essential ingredient for accurate depiction or aircraft or military vehicles.

At this period of his early career Brian said he "went into the technical illustration business with a vengeance." Better qualified to direct a variety of studio

procedures, Brian next became advertising manager for a small studio in Bromley High Street. Despite early enthusiasm for his new job, Brian soon discovered that few of his new colleagues were anywhere near his standard. Apparently the firm was simply unable to recruit staff of the standard blue-chip clients demanded and which the talented Brian aspired to. Disinclined to be held back, Brian decided to strike out as a freelance and he has been self-employed ever since.

At about the same time that Brian decided to go it alone, the US construction kit company established a British subsidiary, Revell (GB). With manufacturing capacity north of London at Potters Bar, the company was headquartered in the capital's Berners Street.

With his interest in aircraft and his facility for technical illustration, Brian decided that Revell, busy introducing a range of aircraft and ship kits into Britain, would make ideal clients. He pestered them relentlessly and

Surviving examples of early box top roughs are exceedingly scarce. Here, artist Brian Knight roughs out the box art for Airfix's HO/OO Arabs.

And here's the final result in colour! The release of this mid-'sixties set was no doubt inspired by the enormous success earlier in the decade of David Lean's 'Lawrence of Arabia'.

was eventually given a commission. He had fallen on his feet and a client–supplier relationship ensued which lasted a dozen years.

At this time Brian began to attend a great many toy and hobby industry trade fairs. Not surprisingly he made contact with Revell's competitors and soon came to the attention of one of the fastest-growing companies – Airfix. However, Brian had more than enough work from Revell, so wasn't desperate for new business. It wasn't until one Eric Robertson, Revell's new

Another Brian Knight box top rough. This time for the Airfix ⅟₃₂nd scale polypropylene 'Russian Infantry' set.

Final box art for the ⅟₃₂nd scale infantry set. Like other Airfix 'soft plastic' figures they aren't strictly kits of course. Nevertheless modellers used these cheap and plentiful figures as an ideal accompaniment in dioramas.

AIRFIX

RUSSIAN INFANTRY
1/32 SCALE

ACTUAL SIZE

MILITARY SERIES

1/32 SCALE

29 SCALE PIECES

Artist Brian Knight with two of his illustrations. He is standing alongside the Supermarine 'SE.6B' in Southampton's Hall of Aviation.

Original Brian Knight art for the Airfix HO/OO 'Astronaut' set. Dating from 1969, the release was timed to coincide with the 'Apollo' moon-launch.

studio manager who had recently joined from Airfix told him of their interest, that he was encouraged to contact the famous British manufacturer. Brian was told that Airfix had a requirement for more artists – especially for their new larger-scale 'Classic Ships' range. Brian's first commission for them was *HMS Endeavour*. Soon, vessels from the age of sail became Brian's speciality. He progressed to produce the stunning artwork for the entire series, including such masterpieces as *Victory*, *Wasa*, *Prince* and *Royal Sovereign*. His last large-scale 'Classic Ship' was the *St. Louis*. Brian told me that he is somewhat disappointed by Airfix's current decision to cut out each ship as a vignette and discard some of the background detail of the original paintings.

As he was getting his teeth into sailing vessels for Airfix, Charlie Smith, the firm's then studio manager

said, "Brian, we are thinking about a new series. What are you like at figures?" Thus began another strand in Brian's career with Airfix and he began to prepare each and every piece of artwork for the entire HO-OO poly-thene figure range. Actually one of the factors that encouraged Airfix to ask Brian to switch to figures was because the firm had run out of subjects for sailing ships! Such was the success of these little and very inexpensive figures that Airfix could barely keep up with the demand. Brian recalls that each artwork was required "Yesterday"!

In fact, such was the pressure generated by the need to feed Airfix with illustration after illustration whilst the company expanded during the 1960s, that even senior Airfix management had to adopt a hands-on role to be sure that every new kit was released on schedule

HO/OO German Infantry (First tooling) in revised box.

Brian Knight's art for the above prior to graphics.

Anonymous artwork for 'Caesar's Gate' Playset.

(remember the days when each month, at least three or four new kits appeared?) Indeed, even the late John Gray, when MD of the kits division, felt inclined to regularly mount dawn raids on his suppliers to check they were working to schedule.

"For example, early in the morning as he made his way to Airfix's Wandsworth offices, John Gray used to knock on the door of my Kent studio to enquire about the progress of *HMS Victory*," Brian recalled. "I said: 'For God's sake, I am working up until 10 o'clock on your work and you are on my doorstep at 7 o'clock the following morning. I need sleep!' Though in a rush, John respected me and left me alone." Such was the pace at Airfix nearly 40 years ago.

Both Roy Cross and Brian Knight regularly travelled by train to present their latest masterpieces to the Airfix management. Brian travelled from Petts Wood in Kent, Roy from Tunbridge Wells. Apparently they often

bumped into each other as they passed through London railway stations; one on their way to – the other returning from – a presentation at Airfix! "I knew Roy Cross very well. We passed each other like ships in the night. He was on the aviation side for Airfix and I was involved with ships and did some figure work," Brian said. When Brian joined Airfix, Roy Cross was already well established with the firm.

Brian was in the enviable position of working for three kit manufacturers at the same time (he clearly didn't need to sleep!) Together with Revell and Airfix, he also worked for Rovex (FROG) based in Margate. In fact he started with FROG on the same day as he secured his first commission from Revell. "I was so excited," recalled Brian. Cruelly, on the same day as he learnt that he had 'won' FROG, his father was diagnosed with cancer.

With business booming, Brian found it hard to keep

up with the demand generated by all three kit companies. "On one occasion, I had so much work on, I simply couldn't sleep for three days if I was to fulfil all the contracts," he told me. Once, on his way back home from a visit to FROG in Margate he was so exhausted that he fell asleep on the train, missed his stop and didn't awake until the train came to a halt in Charing Cross!

Brian told me that a good friend, the late Frank Wooton, was probably his greatest artistic influence. It was Frank Wooton who actually recommended Brian to Colport China and encouraged the artist to pursue a lucrative career undertaking commissions for collectible china.

Brian used to prepare monochrome gouache preliminary 'sketches' for each of his kit box tops. He found that the simple expedient of mixing black and white paint to create a range of tonal values produced illustrations that "enabled me to 'mentally' establish the

Detail from original art for ½nd scale 'Combat Pack'.

Detail from Stalingrad 'Battlefront' Set.

final colour concept of the finished illustration". He also prepared pencil sketches on tracing paper. He preferred working on this substrate because though it enabled sharp lines to be drawn it was equally capable of reproducing subtle shading and a range of tonal values. Brian used the full range of pencils – from HB to 6B.

I think the most memorable work that Brian ever did for Airfix was for the ½nd scale figure range. Here, he truly developed a unique style. Each of these boxes has an illustration of almost cinema poster impact which leads the viewer's eye from two or three figures interacting in the foreground leading back to a dramatic scene that extends beyond the middle distance to a panoramic background. I think these paintings, for which he was paid £125 per box top (they often took a fortnight to complete) were and are very different from the norm. They present a very imaginative way of using the limited space available and are, to my mind, Brian's

signature works.

Together with excellent box art, Airfix are justly recognised for the diversity of their subject matter. The following short selection of classic kits gives an idea of the firm's diversity. In 1965 Airfix secured the licence to produce replicas based on the successful 007 films. Their James Bond & Odd Job diorama from 'Goldfinger' was the initial result. Together with the Wallis Autogiro *Little Nellie* from 'Thunderball' that followed soon after, these kits commanded enormous sums on the 'collectors' market until they were re-released in the 1990s by Humbrol for a fraction of the dealers' price. Speculators beware – as long as they posses the original mould tools, kit manufacturers have an almost infinite capability to release supposedly rare kits. In 1967 Airfix added another 007 classic to their range with the release of James Bond's ejector seat-equipped Aston Martin 'DB5'. To my knowledge, this kit and James Bond's

Original art 54mm 'British Guardsman', 1971.

Original art 54mm 'French Imperial Guard', 1973.

Toyota '2000 GT' have yet to reappear.

Airfix are principally famous for their aircraft kits. The successes of the 1950s meant that the firm could afford to invest in larger injection-moulding machines. The consequence of this was that Airfix were able to produce larger and more complex kits. Even in ½nd – really the smallest 'universal' scale – many bomber and commercial aircraft with large wingspans required substantial tools. With the increased capacity, Airfix was able to meet the demands of eager younger schoolboys with the introduction of RAF Bomber Command's WWII 'Lancaster', 'Halifax' and 'Wellington' bombers. These kits were joined in 1966 by other 'heavies' – the RAF's Short 'Stirling' and the USAAF's 'B-29 Super Fortress' that had a truly awesome wingspan, even in ½nd scale.

The largest Airfix kits appeared in 1970 with the introduction of the massive ¼th scale 'Superkits' range of scale model aircraft. First in the range was a 'Spitfire

AIRFIX-HO-OO SCALE
WWII GERMAN INFANTRY
48 SCALE PIECES

Revised HO/OO W.W.II German Infantry.

Detail from German W.W.II Polythene figures box.

Detail of W.W.II 'British Commandos' Box.

Mk 1'. This kit set new standards for worldwide kit production. It featured removable access panels, which revealed the fighter's eight machine-gun armament and detachable engine cowlings concealing an accurately scaled miniature of the 'Spitfire's' famous Rolls-Royce Merlin engine. For those who wanted more authenticity the model's propeller could be made to turn by the addition of an Airfix 'Spin-a-Prop' electric motor.

Incidentally, at the time of writing, the status of Airfix's legendary association

with model aircraft was again confirmed. This time by a letter that Ray, a keen-eyed pal of mine, spotted in *Private Eye,* the popular British satirical magazine. The letter concerned the accuracy of an Airfix 'Spitfire' that former Conservative leader Iain Duncan Smith was 'allegedly' constructing and had mentioned in 'his' diary. There's no escaping such a famous name!

Together with a demand for bigger and better kits, consumer trends in the 1970s also encouraged a big growth in military modelling – especially in the field of model soldiers. To satisfy this demand, in 1971 Airfix introduced the first of a new range of 54mm 'Collectors' model soldiers, a British Guardsman from the Napoleonic period.

Testament to Airfix's commitment to military modelling in the 1970s and especially to the 'traditional' British model soldier scale of 54mm was the

James Bond Toyota '2000 GT', 1968.

Airfix working 'Super Hovercraft' from the late 1970s – testament to the firm's confidence and diversity by this time.

Lotus 'Cortina', 1969.

VW 'Beetle', 1964.

Airfix 'Data Car', 1980. Complete 'with built-in electronic memory' – but how much? Certainly a fraction of what today's computer-literate youngsters enjoy on even the simplest PC game!

Spitfire

Classic Aircraft No.1
Their history and how to model them

by **Roy Cross** and Gerald Scarborough

The first in the *Classic Aircraft* range written by Roy Cross and Gerald Scarborough.

introduction of a fairly highly detailed 'toy' range of ready-assembled military vehicles. These series included the British army's then new Alvis 'Stalwart' amphibious vehicle and the artillery's powerful 'Abbot' SP gun along with some rather curiously chosen German 'adversaries' from WWII! The scale chosen for these miniatures was the direct equivalent of 54mm – 1/32nd scale. At around the time of the introduction of their ready-assembled tank and vehicle range, Airfix introduced a series of construction kits in the same scale. They already had a well-established range of 00/H0 military vehicles, mostly tanks, introduced in the 1960s to accompany their famous polythene soldier sets. First in this excellent range was Airfix's finely detailed replica of General Montgomery's 'Snipe' staff car – 'Monty's Humber' – that appeared in 1972.

In the same scale, Airfix added other superb replicas to the range. These included a model of the half-

1/72nd scale 'Dambusting' Avro Lancaster from 617 Sq.

1/72nd scale Harrier GR-7

tracked personal vehicle used by Rommel, Monty's famous German opposite number in the western desert, and representations of Britain's 'Crusader' and 'M3 Grant' tanks, also from the El Alamein period. Unfortunately, ⅟₃₂ scale was rather the odd-man-out in the field of military modelling, a genre which was rapidly being dominated by Japanese manufacturers, principally Tamiya. Airfix's competitors had adopted ⅟₃₅th scale, which was also more popular in the USA. The incompatibility between scales, which prevented modellers from converting or adapting spare parts between kits from different manufacturers meant that ⅟₃₂nd scale – for tanks and vehicles at least – was destined to fail. If you can't beat them join them, and ultimately Airfix were forced to chose ⅟₃₅th. However, because they had to do so in a hurry, or risk losing market share, they were forced to purchase some mould tools from Japanese manufacturer Max and re-badge them as Airfix products.

By the mid-1970s Airfix had more or less conquered every area of plastic kit construction from aircraft to cars and ships through railways, model soldiers, military vehicles, large ⅟₁₂th scale 'famous people' from history figures and numerous science fact and fiction models. On top of this, of course, Airfix Plastics had a large toy and craft range. The Airfix Group itself comprised a roll call of the most famous names in the British toy and model industry, including the famous model brand itself, which like 'Hoover' had actually become synonymous with any product from its own industry, and equally respected names like Meccano, Dinky, Triang, and Pedigree.

Confident enough in 1975 to take a full-page advertisement in the *Financial Times*, under the heading 'Another Record Year', Chairman Ralph Ehrmann said "Never has such a short period of time so enhanced our potential." In the 1974/75 financial year Airfix Industries turnover was up 38 per cent and profits had leapt a staggering 30 per cent.

It seemed that nothing could stop Airfix, but little did Ralph Ehrmann and his MD know, trouble was looming.

The Airfix group of companies entered the 1980s with gradually accumulating problems. Although the kit division was still profitable, Meccano and Dinky were in trouble. Because of the cross-guarantee nature of the group structure, trouble within individual divisions quickly reverberated around the entire group. The knock-on effect of problems to the complex financial interlacing, essential to funding investment and providing cash-flow, was a cumulative disaster. Exports were down, which further limited cash.

Airfix products ceased trading in January 1981. Cruel irony dictated that the announcement of this sudden misfortune was made at the 1981 Earls Court Toy Fair.

Titled "Airfix Mirrors Depression", an article in the *Financial Times* from 30 January 1981, written by journalist David Churchill, read: "On the eve of the toy industry's annual

⅟₃₂nd scale North American P-51 D/K Mustang in Swedish markings

45

**Airfix HO/OO scale
'Jungle Headquarters'.**

trade fair, which opens at London's Earls Court tomorrow, Airfix Industries was yesterday finally forced to call in receivers."

His article, some of which I've reproduced below, gives the reader a very good impression of the tumult through which Airfix was trying to navigate.

"The development has been likely for the past 12 months as Airfix has struggled to stay solvent in a notoriously fickle business. Pre-Christmas toy spending – traditionally the industry's most important time – was unimpressive, even though low stockholdings by many retailers gave the impression that sales were good."

"With the recession continuing, and unemployment increasing, the outlook for toy spending this year is already gloomy. Exhibition space at tomorrow's fair is down by some 10 per cent and few exhibitors can feel at all buoyant about the prospects for 1981."

"Airfix, however, has been fairly bullish in recent weeks about its prospects, pointing to a revamped

**Airfix HO/OO scale
'Forward Command Post'.**

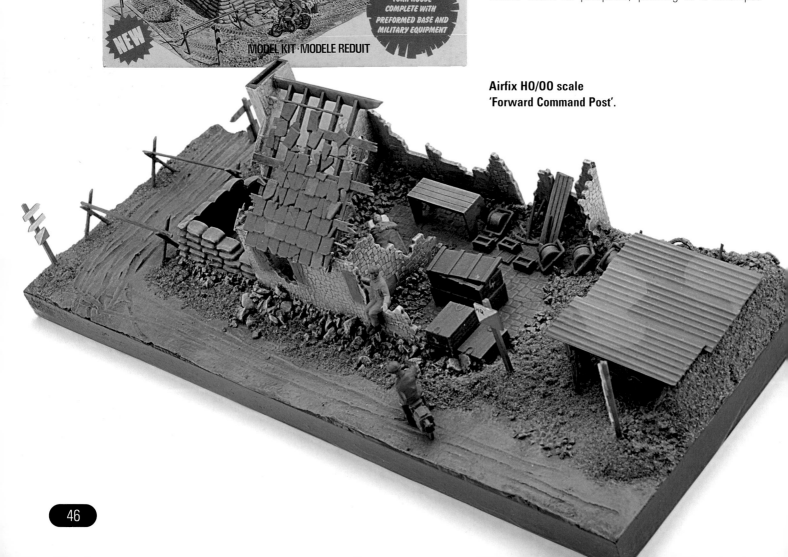

product range and claiming that its December sales were a record for the company."

The article went on to suggest that because wholesalers had let their stock of kits dwindle, the company might soon expect some hefty orders, but it was pessimistic about the future:

"In November, Airfix published its much-delayed financial results for 1979–80. These showed a pre-tax loss of £2.1m even before factory closures. These were followed in December by the interim figures showing a loss of £2.35m for the six months leading to end September on a decline in turnover from £11.8m to £11.3m."

"These results came after a year in which the company had struggled to reduce its bank borrowings. Just before Christmas 1979, Airfix closed its Liverpool-based Meccano factory with the loss of 900 jobs."

"The closure, a severe blow in an area of high unemployment, was contested by trade unions and MPs and managed to absorb much of the company's management time. Stockbrokers, Grieveson Grant, suggest that, 'had the Meccano closure proceeded smoothly the group would be in a stronger position'. In a further move to raise money to reduce its borrowings, Airfix sold its

profitable Crayonne and Declon plastics companies last November for £4.7m."

The day before the article appeared, Airfix issued a statement saying that it had "put forward proposals to its UK bankers for a financial reconstruction of the group", but unfortunately these had been unsuccessful. Ralph Ehrmann, Airfix's chairman, said that Airfix was "very surprised the banks were not prepared to accept the proposals as presented. They seemed very reasonable to us and our advisers." Consequently, Airfix had no option but to request a share suspension and to call in receivers.

The receivers continued to administer Airfix group businesses while they reviewed operations and sought buyers for the various Airfix divisions. "They aim to sell the various businesses as going concerns," said the *Financial Times*.

The 'Airfield Control Tower' originated in 1959 as a railway accessory. In the 1970s it reappeared for use in aircraft dioramas.

Fine Gavin Macleod artwork for the Airfix ¹/₁₄₄th 'F-104 Starfighter'.

Gavin Macleod's interpretation of Airfix's ¹/₇₂nd scale Junkers 'Ju-87B Stuka'.

As the article made clear, Airfix wasn't the sole casualty of negative market pressures in the British toy industry. It reminded readers that only the previous year the famous British firms, Dunbee-Combex-Marx and Lesney were in trouble – the former calling in the receiver like Airfix and Lesney, the originators of 'Matchbox' cars, being forced to shed some 1,300 jobs. "Pressures on the industry face British industry in general. These include out-dated products, soaring sterling, rising imports, and a foreign stranglehold on vital new technology," wrote Mr Churchill.

The rather gloomy *Financial Times* article did end on a high note as far as Airfix is concerned: "However, Airfix has some bright spots since there is wide acceptance of the quality of its products," concluded the

Airfix BAe Red Arrows 'Hawks' (¹⁄₄₈th). Gavin Macleod.

feature. "But whether they can be produced cheaply enough to compete with overseas competition is a question that any potential buyer will have to consider."

Fortunately all was not lost and the famous Airfix brand was destined for survival. In 1981, outbidding Britain's Humbrol, who had long coveted Airfix, Palitoy, part of US Giant General Mills and famous as the British manufacturer of 'Action Man', the British equivalent of America's 'GI-Joe', plucked them from the limbo of receivership.

Shipping surviving Airfix moulds to their production plant in Calais, Palitoy audited the entire range under the heading 'List of A.F.T.O. (Airfix Take Over) Moulds'. So, beginning on 22 April 1981, Airfix classics such as the 00/HO 'RAF Refuelling Set' (acquisition cost: £2,000) and the new ¹⁄₇₂nd scale 'MiG 23 Flogger' (acquisition cost: £11,800 which gives some idea of their relative importance to a new owner), began their journey to the continent, where ironically they remain today, but more of that later.

Airfix's transfer of ownership to Palitoy wasn't a bad fit. Two years previously Palitoy had celebrated their diamond jubilee. Established by Alfred Pallett as

¹⁄₄₈th scale BAe 'Harrier GR3'.

Cascelloid Ltd in 1919 to exploit the new market for celluloid, the company manufactured a dazzling array of household articles. After exploring the potential of toy manufacture Cascelloid began the manufacture of toy dolls in 1925 and began to expand their interests in the children's market, registering the trademark Palitoy in 1935. Immediately after the Second World War Palitoy were able to demonstrate the first vinyl injection moulding of toy cars – to King George VI and Queen Elizabeth no less. In 1968 one of Britain's major industrial concerns, British Xylonite Company Ltd (BXL), who had

Airfix ¹⁄₄₈th scale Supermarine 'Spitfire MkVIIIc'.

bought Cascelloid in 1931, sold Palitoy to General Mills Inc. By 1979 General Mills had grown into the world's No. 1 toy conglomerate. Airfix appeared to be in good company indeed.

In the early 1980s, whilst American-owned, decisions about forthcoming kit releases were shared with Airfix's North American sister company, M.P.C., also owned by General Mills. This explains why so many Airfix releases from the 1980s, such as the 'Star Wars' series of models, were also separately available as M.P.C. kits. Today Britain's Humbrol, who finally acquired Airfix in 1986, having earlier been outbid by General Mills and buying French kit manufacturer Heller in an effort to complete their hobby supplies portfolio, have only themselves to please.

As soon as a subject for a new model has been agreed, some three to four months of intensive product design work begins. Then, another three months are scheduled

for pattern making and as much as ten months allocated for tool making. Packaging design and commissioning the box top artist, designing and writing the instruction leaflet and production of the all-important decals (if included) runs concurrently with the tool-making phase. Combined, it takes at least a year and as much as 18 months before a kit idea actually reaches the shops.

Today the pace of kit release at Airfix is a fraction of what it once was. With tooling costs so fabulously expensive, like some other manufacturers the trend at Airfix is for mould-share – re-boxing kits which have appeared in other ranges (such as many of Airfix's more recent ¹⁄₄₈th releases which were tooled by Japanese manufacturer Otaki). Fortunately, however, the famous Airfix logo can still be found aplenty in model shops and, as the kit brand enters its sixth decade, it remains Britain's greatest name in plastic construction kits. The story moves on.

Sadly, since publication of my 50th anniversary commemoration of Airfix in 1990, one of the major players from the 'old days' has left us.

John Gray, one of the prime movers behind Airfix kits, died in November 2000. He was 80 years old.

John will need little introduction to Airfix aficionados. Fans know that part of the company's initial success was down to his desire for scale accuracy and his love of aircraft – two passions he shared with Airfix's 'busi-

ness brain', Ralph Ehrmann. However, I know Ralph would be the first to acknowledge John's particular role in encouraging Airfix to achieve new levels of excellence within the rapidly developing British injection-moulding industry.

John Gray involved himself in the minutiae of kit production and was as interested in box art as he was in mould tool design. Airfix artist Brian Knight told me that whilst on his way to work, John frequently called into

Gavin Macleod's interpretation of Airfix's venerable ¹⁄₇₂nd scale Westland 'Sea King'.

¹⁄₇₂nd scale RAF Avro 'Vulcan B Mk2' in the South Atlantic, 1982.

Brian's Kent studio to enquire about the progress of a particular illustration. At times this interference irritated Brian, who, like most artists, wanted to be left to work in solitude. However, they soon became firm friends and Brian realised that John simply cared. Fellow artistic supremo Roy Cross showed me surviving examples of pencil 'box top roughs', each emblazoned with either a bold 'Yes!' or 'No!' in John's distinctive hand. Such recollections are testament to his involvement.

John Gray joined Airfix from Lines Bros, where he was a buyer. Initially he fulfilled a similar role at Airfix, but soon rose to be general manager of the firm. Ralph Ehrmann told me about the volatility of Airfix founder

Nicholas Kove and how in the early days he often undermined John Gray and other senior Airfix colleagues. "Very shortly John and I became very close," Ralph told me. "When I first joined Airfix, there were two or three times when I had to stop John resigning. I'm sure that having John there helped me to carry on too," he said.

Every year Airfix would introduce new features such as optional parts and alternative liveries. They generally led where others followed and Airfix quickly became synonymous with value for money. Many such innovations were initiated or encouraged by John Gray. Modellers owe him a round of thanks.

Gavin Macleod art for Airfix's Saab 'AJ-37 Viggen', one of the firm's newer ¹⁄₁₄₄th scale offerings.

Fortunately, Ralph Ehrmann is still very much with us. Though no longer involved with Airfix, typically Ralph is still involved with business and some very 21st-century ones at that. Despite his official retirement from industry, Ralph Ehrmann has become heavily involved with Cashbacs International, a leading-edge supplier of automated bank transfer systems established in 1987 and now sponsored by banking giant HSBC as an approved BACS bureau.

In January 1999, in the sumptuous surroundings of the Great Hall of Lincoln's Inn, shortly after the Toy Fair, Ralph Ehrmann was honoured for his outstanding contribution to the toy industry. At the British Toy & Hobby Association's fourth Roll of Honour Dinner, Ralph Ehrmann was presented with a specially commissioned bronze casting created by famous sculpture and figure modeller, Ron Cameron. As enthusiasts will know, coincidentally, Ron Cameron was one of the sculptors behind the master patterns of Airfix's model figure range.

This book is principally about the history and development of the plastic kit industry in general and the recent fashion in collecting old and out of production kits. An international market has developed with traders and dealers publishing lists of hundreds of mouth-watering rarities from yesteryear offered from a few pounds to many hundreds. A pristine Airfix Ferguson tractor might set you back a thousand pounds today and other rare Airfix kits are most collectible.

The fact that kit collecting has gained currency with experts is proved by recent media interest on the subject. Following publication of my aforementioned history of Airfix I was invited to present a section about collecting Airfix kits on British TV.

Recorded at Roy Cross's house in April 2000, the Airfix feature was actually broadcast on Channel 4's Collectors' Lot (a 'Two Four Production') in November the same year. Robert Smith was the presenter.

Despite having never seen it previously, I had some misgivings about the programme. I guess I was expecting a rather tongue-in-cheek satire along the lines of 'Here's Arthur – the test pilot for Airfix'. Robert's 'to camera' introduction, "Let's dive bomb into a subject

Entire panorama of Gavin Macleod's art for the ½nd scale Westland 'Navy Lynx Mk8'.

dear to many men's hearts," didn't inspire much confidence either. I was, however, relieved when he confessed to being a collector himself – not of kits but of … chairs (and they say model fans are weird!) Apparently he buys classic furniture by designers like Charles Eames and Marcel Breuer. This revelation and the care with which the Production Company handled some of the more fragile examples from my collection quickly reassured me. I soon discovered that the programmers were sincere and not out for cheap laughs. Hopefully, the finished programme revealed their serious intent.

After turning a corner of poor Roy's studio into a 'shrine to Airfix' (lots of my kits piled atop a trestle table and flanked by Roy's original art and yet more kits) I was carefully positioned before the camera and encouraged to recall my fondest memories of Airfix. I was asked to explain precisely why and how I collect discontinued Airfix kits. Those lucky enough to see the programme might recall my somewhat disembodied head peering from behind a mound of classic old kits.

Humbrol's Trevor Snowden had thoughtfully driven all the way down from Hull, bringing with him a bevy of current kits in varying states of assembly – thereby precisely demonstrating the kit construction process. Trevor was also able to unveil some Airfix newcomers which, as real enthusiasts will know, largely consist of licensed produced moulds like the ex-Otaki ⅟₄₈th scale aircraft (though these are very good indeed). He was able to show us early examples of the retooled ⅟₂₄th scale 'Harrier' now available in G3 guise.

Like me, Roy Cross was also put through the mill in front of the television camera. He was asked to explain how he brought the contents of the average Airfix box – some 40 or 50 small pieces of white, light grey or pale blue polystyrene – to life. He told viewers how he managed to create stunning artworks, which suggested infinite possibilities to the young imagination. He also described the process from box top rough to final artwork and took great pains to explain how he tackled the awkward 'letterbox' proportions of the average Airfix kit box – something I know Roy has always felt limited the

"Steady, steady …" Airfix 'Seafire' coming in to land. Another classic from the late Gavin Macleod.

potential of his paintings. To be honest, Roy's performance suggested an entire programme dedicated to the box top artist's craft.

I have received a good few letters since my appearance on 'Collectors' Lot'. Some have come from unashamed enthusiasts and many from lapsed modellers who were spurred by the sight of so much 'Airfixania' into trotting to their local toyshop to buy an Airfix starter kit. Good for them! Many 40-something contemporaries of mine were relieved to come out of the closet in the happy realisation that they were in the company of lots of other over-grown schoolboys who couldn't escape all of their childhood passions.

What the programme managed to do, however briefly, was to transport sympathetic viewers back to an imagined halcyon time when, in exchange for 2/-, they could embark upon an exciting journey into an imaginary realm in which they controlled and led squadrons of fighter aircraft, flotillas of destroyers or troops of armoured fighting vehicles in pursuit of a vanquished enemy. To echo veteran enthusiast John Wells – Airfix is after all "about childhood".

Finally, in this section about Airfix, enthusiasts might like to learn briefly some more information gleaned since the publication of my first book about the company. They relate to former Airfix factories and their survival and occupation today.

Haldane Place, the famous Airfix plant in Earlsfield, South London, survives today as a modern converted business complex. Previously, together with Airfix's design and manufacturing HQ, it was where all 'modellers of a certain age' posted complaint slips requesting the return of a missing or broken part.

Incidentally, today manufacturers have got wise to the fact that most of these requests are simply to help stock modellers, 'spare parts boxes'. Revell-Monogram for example minutely weigh each kit before despatch, so they know precisely if the contents is complete – be warned!

From 1949 to 1981, the products that filled the spare time of innumerable schoolboys (and their Dads) were made on the site of what is today landlord 'Workspace's'

Airfix ¹⁄₄₈th scale 'Buccaneer'.

JUST LIKE THE REAL THING!

The 66,000-ton "France" is the longest liner in the world, carries 2,000 passengers and a crew of 1,000. Launched in 1962, it cost almost £30,000,000 to build. This superb 1/600 scale model will make a wonderful companion to the Airfix "Queen Elizabeth" and "Canberra" 148-part kit—only 10/6. There are over 200 Airfix Kits covering 13 different series. And at 2/- to 17/6 you can well afford to make all your models *just like the real thing!*

AIRFIX CONSTANT SCALE
CONSTRUCTION KITS
Just like the real thing!
From model and hobby shops, toy shops and F. W. Woolworth

STOP PRESS

ROLAND C11
A realistic model of the World War 1 German fighter, known as 'the whale'. Complete with crew and swivelling guns, the kit includes special distinctive transfer markings. 31 part kit. 2/-

Also new Airacobra American Ground Attack fighter. 37 part kit. 2/-

Printed by Oxley & Son (Windsor) Ltd., 2-4 Victoria Street, Windsor

Press ad for Airfix's kit of the enormous liner, *S.S. France*. This is now one of the rarest Airfix kits as it is one of the few models for which the mould tool no longer exists.

previously occupied by Ediswan light bulbs. This building dated from about 1900 and had originally been an abattoir. Airfix then bought the building in about 1953, and subsequently acquired a laundry, a sweet factory, a Martini bottling plant and various other 'metal-bashing' concerns. The company's building (now demolished and replaced by a DIY store) that stood at the top of Haldane Place, at the junction with Garratt Lane, carried the Airfix name and logo on its roof.

Ralph Ehrmann recalled that "most of the workforce lived in the immediate vicinity of the factory – it was very much a local company, as were most of the many factories in Earlsfield and Wandsworth at that time. Some of the skilled tool-makers lived a little further afield in Earlsfield and towards Clapham."

Initially, all this, and the assembly and packaging as well, took place at Haldane Place. Subsequently Airfix set up a warehouse in nearby Ravensbury Road – one local resident remembers going there each week to collect a dozen or 20 models to make up for shop displays, a useful source of extra cash. In 1973 additional moulding and assembly facilities were established in a former tram depot in Charlton to meet increasing demand.

Interestingly, at the time of writing, a work colleague showed me an item on the internet which described the redevelopment of the Greenwich Peninsula Airfix site into a modern commercial retail park. "Redevelopment of this brown field old industrial site that was heavily polluted, required careful consideration," the article read. "Up to 4m of made ground contaminated with volatile organic chemicals and coal ash had been tipped on the Charlton Marshes early in the 20th century for a tram depot followed by an Airfix factory."

I find the phrase "an Airfix factory" rewarding. It suggests that, after all this time, in Britain at least, the brand name is still as synonymous with model kits as 'Hoover' is with vacuum cleaners.

Riverside Business Centre. Haldane Place and Bendon Valley, the next road to the north, were (and remain) narrow, unprepossessing streets of terraced housing and small factories and workshops terminating on the banks of the River Wandle.

Ralph Ehrmann, chairman of Airfix Industries throughout the Haldane Place years, remembers that, to begin with, the company rented a 14,000 square foot factory

Bringing the Airfix story as up to date as I can, I must mention the firm's recent change of ownership (Airfix fans are getting used to this!) In May 2003 a press release stated that: "Hobby Products Group (Holdings) Limited, the Holding Company for the Group including the famous names of Airfix, Humbrol, Joustra & Heller, has a new controlling stakeholder, Business Development Group ('BDG')."

BDG said that they had acquired the stake as part of a management review of the Group and foresaw the move would help it to further develop Airfix, *et al*, as a "major force in the hobby and leisure market." Humbrol's response was equally upbeat. They said they were "delighted to see such a major commitment from BDG in terms of their confidence in the future growth prospects of the Group" and looked forward to building on the success already achieved. Naturally, Airfix devotees worldwide would echo these sentiments.

The Airfix design office outing to Paris in 1964. It allegedly cost £14 10/- each. John Gray gave each employee an additional half-day holiday and said that he wished he was coming too. From left: Peter Allen, John Edwards and Mike Mason. Apparently, Mike was one of the product designers who had a penchant for mould design – Peter favoured component design, so they often swapped these elements with each other!

Upon his retirement from Airfix, John Gray (second from left) is presented with a travelling clock by Chairman Ralph Ehrmann. Fellow directors O.V. Hoare (left) and F.D.G. Norburn look on.

Titled Airfix 'Present ¹⁄₂₄th scale Harrier', the original caption to this picture from May 1974 reads:
"During recent months Airfix have been working in close co-operation with the Royal Air Force and No.1 Fighter Squadron in particular to produce their latest ¹⁄₂₄th scale Superkit – 'Harrier GR.1'. As soon as the first production model became available Airfix Technical Researcher, Barry Wheeler, got to work and built the first ¹⁄₂₄th scale model of this famous aircraft."

Picture shows: Wing Commander P.P.W. Taylor, O/C No.1(F) Squadron, Royal Air Force Wittering being presented with the first 'Harrier' model by Barry Wheeler (right) while Airfix draughtsman Peter Allen (centre) looks on. The presentation took place on the airfield with one of the squadron's operational aircraft in the background.

AMT

I'm sure that most plastic kit enthusiasts know that 'AMT' – three letters that signify one of the greatest names in model car and truck construction kits – is derived from this American company's original name, 'Aluminum Model Toy Company'. Those who didn't know this have learnt something!

Although AMT, which began making construction kits shortly after the Second World War, released many aircraft kits in the late 1960s (mostly re-boxed FROG and Hasegawa originals), the company is justly famous for its automobile models. AMT's range is enormous and includes everything from their first ever all-plastic car kit, a 1953 convertible Ford 'Indy Pace Car' in ⅕th scale and the memorable 1960 'Edsel Ford' to more modern classics such as 1977's 'Kiss Custom Chevy Van' which came complete with decals of the US Glam Rockers clad in catsuits, face-paint and outlandish platform-soled boots.

Like most other North American kit manufacturers who fuelled that nation's insatiable demand for models of the latest production coupés or show cars, AMT also caught the 'far-out' wave of Flower Power and produced many outlandish custom vehicles, characteristic of the late 1960s. Personal favourites include the 1960s ⅕th scale 'Lil Roamin' Chariot', which came complete with stylised bodywork which suggested it was Spartacus on wheels, and 'Royal Rail', a ⅕th scale dragster from 1970 which cocked a snook at supposed British pomposity by including a seat and cockpit arrangement shaped like a Monarch's crown!

In 1978 Britain's Lesney, owners of the 'Matchbox' brand, purchased AMT. A few years later AMT's tools were in turn acquired by the ERTL Corporation and most recently they have become the property of die-cast manufacturer, Racing Champions.

Snap-together AMT 'Batskiboat' from 'Batman Returns' movie.

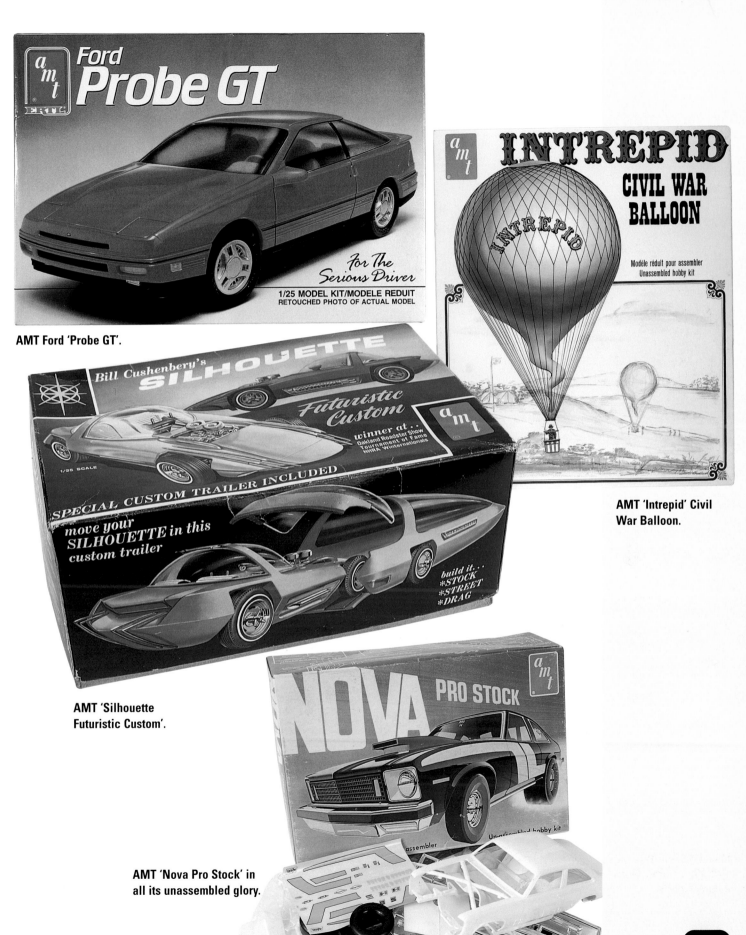

Ford Probe GT

For The Serious Driver

1/25 MODEL KIT/MODELE REDUIT
RETOUCHED PHOTO OF ACTUAL MODEL

AMT Ford 'Probe GT'.

INTREPID CIVIL WAR BALLOON

Modèle réduit pour assembler
Unassembled hobby kit

AMT 'Intrepid' Civil War Balloon.

Bill Cushenbery's **SILHOUETTE**

Futuristic Custom

winner at . . .
Oakland Roadster Show
Tournament of Fame
NHRA Winternationals

1/25 SCALE

SPECIAL CUSTOM TRAILER INCLUDED

move your SILHOUETTE *in this* custom trailer

build it . . .
*STOCK
*STREET
*DRAG

AMT 'Silhouette Futuristic Custom'.

NOVA PRO STOCK

Unassembled hobby kit

AMT 'Nova Pro Stock' in all its unassembled glory.

AURORA PLASTICS
OF BROOKLYN, NEW YORK

Aurora began life in 1950 when Americans Abe Shikes, John Cuomo and Joe Giammarino rented small premises in Brooklyn, New York. Led by Shikes, a GI who had returned from active service and decided to invest his pre-war talents in sales into a new plastic manufacturing venture, the trio energetically exploited any opportunity to turn an honest profit.

An early success, which illustrates their imaginative spirit, occurred when Aurora purchased a job lot of failed coat hangers that were too narrow to securely support heavy garments. With the bravado that characterised its early days, Aurora simply converted the useless plastic items into inexpensive bow and arrow sets for kids! Production costs were diligently kept to a minimum. In return for crates of cold beer, off-duty firemen were employed to tie the bowstrings.

During its first two years, Aurora survived by making a disparate range of household goods and toys.

The breakthrough came in 1952 when Shikes was buying birdseed in a local general store. Noticing some new plastic kits, of the type Aurora were perfectly capable of producing, he was amazed to discover the apparently high price being charged for them. Returning to Aurora's offices, he convinced his colleagues that the kit business might be the way ahead.

So, reducing the scale and number of component parts, Aurora set about making models similar to the premium-priced ones Shikes had seen earlier.

Their first kit was a replica of a Grumman 'Panther' – one of the new breed of US jet fighters that had caught the mood of the times and about which no self-respecting American schoolboy was ignorant. It was 75 per cent cheaper than the larger model of the same machine with which Shikes had decided to compete head-on. Not surprisingly, Aurora's kit better appealed to the pockets of young consumers and the company immediately followed its first release with another jet fighter kit, this time a model of Lockheed's new 'F-90'.

Both kits were packaged in boxes which featured innovations. Firstly, the price (99 cents) was litho printed as an integral part of

⅛th scale 'US Sailor', 1957.

the box art and, secondly, each kit was shrink wrapped in transparent plastic. The former feature prevented wholesalers and retailers price setting, offering consumers an honest price, and the latter development meant that purchasers could take their new models home, secure in the knowledge that the contents hadn't been tampered with and that all the parts were included. Shrink-wrapping kits is now common practice.

Both kits sold extremely well and Aurora was forced to expand its operations and move to bigger premises in a re-developed bakery nearby.

In 1954 with a dozen items now in their catalogue and profits on the increase, Aurora moved yet again. This time, however, they enjoyed the luxury of a purpose-built facility housing 12 modern injection-moulding machines.

Aurora was a very pleasant working environment, and the management of Shikes as President and Vice Presidents Giammarino and Cuomo steered the company with a gentle benevolence, ensuring that staff enjoyed all modern benefits.

By the early 1960s Aurora had sales of around $20 million. Financial success could only be partly attributed to conventional plastic construction kits, however, because the company's revenues had been boosted by income

from slot car racing products, Aurora being one of the earliest American operators to invest in a popular craze that had developed in Britain. Aurora model kits, often marketed under the brand 'Playcraft Toys', did particularly well in Britain – it was definitely a reciprocal trade.

Another key to their rapid growth was Aurora's growing list of figure kits. Probably the most successful of these – which began with a small range of polystyrene figure models representing each of America's traditional fighting men – was Aurora's famous monster range. These ghoulish creations, each based on an infamous

¹⁄₃₂nd scale Ford 'T Dragster'.

Aurora Roman Bireme.

¼₂th scale 'Mr Spock', 1972.

creature from movie history, had enormous appeal with youngsters. They are probably Aurora's most famous range and had enormous crossover appeal, and, being simple to construct, they were bought by enthusiasts and non-modellers. A 40-something American friend of mine, Ed, grew up in Boston during the 1960s. Like most well-balanced characters he abandoned plastic kits when he entered his teens. However, as I was wittering on to him with stories about kit companies, he suddenly perked up when I mentioned the name 'Aurora'.

Like thousands of American kids in the 60s, Ed remembered having many of Aurora's 'Famous Movie Monsters'. He remembered two kits in particular – 'The Witch', illustrated in Aurora's advertising stirring a boiling cauldron to which she was adding live rats, behind the slogan "Look what Aurora has cooked up now – Mrs Black Magic herself", and 'The Bride of

Frankenstein' ("Here comes the bride"). Each kit retailed for $1.49.

Together with Aurora's famous range of medieval knights like the well-known and very collectible 'Silver Knight of Augsburg', the manufacturers long association with D.C.Comics – on the pages of whose pulps Aurora booked regular press ads to promote model replicas of the very heroes shown on the covers – spawned the range of models for which the firm is most famous, Figure kits, which were really the high point of Aurora's success. Indeed, so popular are they that many of the kits are available today.

When Aurora ceased trading in 1978, Monogram purchased many of their moulds, reissuing them under their own banner. Figure kits such as 'King Kong', 'Batman', 'Superman', 'Frankenstein', 'Dracula', 'Wolf man' and 'Godzilla' enjoyed a new lease of life with Monogram, as did almost the entire range of 'Dinosaurs' – including the 'Giant Woolly Mammoth', which, in model form at least, shared the stage with pre-history's giant reptilians.

All collectors want to learn which kits from the famous manufacturers are the rarest and consequently most valuable. Well, during the transfer of mould tools westwards from New York to Monogram's home outside Chicago, certain Aurora moulds suffered irreparable

¼₈th scale 'Centurion' tank, 1970s.

Fokker 'E.III'.

damage in a rail freight accident. The author has to thank John Burns of the Kit Collectors Clearing House, and possibly the world's most knowledgeable kit enthusiast, for supplying details of which kit moulds were trashed. They are the 'Aero Jet Commander', 'Albatros C.III', 'Halberstadt C.L.II', 'Brequet XIV' and 'Cessna Skymaster'. If you find these kits in their original packaging, think carefully before making them. Ironically, as with other collectible models, they are worth more unmade than assembled.

Collectors will be grateful for the activity of US toy company 'Playing Mantis', and specifically the actions of its cleverly named 'Polar Lights' kit brand (a play on 'Aurora Borealis' – geddit?), for they have taken it upon themselves to re-release many of Aurora's classic scale models. These include many of their figures from films and TV shows, such as 'James Bond', 'Lost In Space' and 'The Man from U.N.C.L.E.'

I understand that Polar Lights, who reproduce ex-Aurora models under an arrangement with Revell-Monogram who now own most of the tools, have perfected a process whereby they can actually recreate the original model without having to resort to the original heavy steel mould-tool. Apparently they use a process that reverses the original procedure and actual-

ly enables a new tool to be cut using surviving moulded parts from the original unassembled kit, as long as they remain in pristine condition. Who knows, perhaps they will furnish modellers with replicas of the 'missing' five aircraft mentioned above?

Mint and boxed Boeing 'F4B-4'.

Quarter scale 'DH10' Bomber by Aurora Playcraft.

Keen eyed readers will notice that the Nieuport cost 39p in Woolworth's in the mid-1970s.

BANDAI

1974
CATALOGUE

BANDAI MODEL KITS

Bandai 1974 catalogue.

Japanese and other Far-Eastern kit manufacturers have long recognised the commercial advantages of diversification. Although Tamiya is renowned as perhaps the best kit company in the world, it does not depend entirely on its plastic model business. Profits are evenly spread between model construction kits and radio control (RC) cars and, more recently, military vehicles. Indeed, relative newcomer Dragon produces parallel product lines with its substantial model kit operation operating alongside an increasingly successful range of ⅙th scale articulated military figures, designed in the Action Man/GI-Joe mould but aimed at collectors, not kids.

Bandai, like Tamiya, is a Japanese company that has also successfully built a business across a range of business areas. Today Bandai is the top-selling toy manufacturer in Japan with a range of market-leading products such as 'Gundam', 'Power Rangers' and 'Digimon'. Each has conspired to make it a global giant. More recently the company has diversified into the entertainment and leisure fields with operations ranging from confectionery and vending equipment to computer, video and DVD software and even children's toiletries!

Incidentally the original company name, 'Bandai-Ya', derives from a Chinese Zhou Dynasty manual of military strategy which, when translated into Japanese, means 'eternally unchanging', a concept the late Naoharu Yamashina, who founded the company, felt appropriate for an organisation intent on bringing joy to youngsters regardless of their nationality or circumstance.

Yamashina started Bandai in July 1950 and his company began life selling a range of celluloid and metal toys. It also did well with a range of rubber swimming rings aimed at the domestic market. However, within a few months Bandai was marketing its own products and by 1955 had expanded sufficiently to require new offices with in-house Research and Development, manufacturing and distribution operations.

Following the enormous success of its 'Cars of the World' range, own-brand slot racing systems (a craze which swept the world in the early 60s) and especially a particularly popular remote-control toy car product, Bandai had outgrown even these premises and was forced to move again. This time Bandai hit gold with its 'AstroBoy' product range — the company's first TV-Character

Delightfully 'deformed' McDonnel-Douglas F-15A Eagle by Bandai. Very similar to the bizarre 'Egg Craft' range of aircraft caricatures released by Hasegawa in the 1970s.

Some more great kits from the mid-1970s.

'RX-78' figure, one of the Mobile Suits (MS) developed by the rival forces of the 'Earth Federation' and its adversaries in the 'Principality of Zeon'. Actually 'Gundam', made a debut on Japanese TV in 1979. It was the idea of director Yoshiyuki Tomino and 'Hajime Yatate', the pen name of all those artists at Sunrise Studios, the animation studio Bandai bought outright in 1994. Since then, 'Gundam' has become one of Bandai's most significant product lines and by July 1999 the firm had sold an outstanding 300 million 'Gundams'!

With a name for producing a large and very successful toy range (many of them aimed at the lucrative pre-school and early teens market) and with numerous 'Power Ranger', 'Gundam', 'Tamagotchi' (how many other dads remember forking out for these 'cyber pets'?), 'Bratz', 'Betty Spaghetti' and, most recently, 'Digimon' toys to its credit, Bandai is a true giant.

However, other than for its earlier military miniatures range, today Bandai is perhaps best known with model enthusiasts as a manufacturer of science-fiction kits. Recently, the company released a superb replica of the original TV version of Star Trek's *USS Enterprise* that was launched simultaneously in six countries including Japan, Korea and the United States. The mouldings of this all-singing-all-dancing kit are pre-coloured and, when assembled, enclose a complex range of fibre-optic filaments which enable purchasers to illuminate the finished model with an array of interior and navigation lights all to scale and guaranteed to make this, not inexpensive, masterpiece the talk of any collection.

toy and the forerunner of many subsequent pan-media tie-ins.

Bandai Models was established in 1971 and very quickly caught the attention of modellers and hobbyists worldwide with a superb range of ⅟₄₈th scale military vehicles and accessories.

Very rapidly, Bandai exploited the enormous success of this range by producing accessory sets and various figures, enabling enthusiasts to complete realistic diorama settings to display their models.

Although Bandai's prolific range of military models is a landmark in the company's development for many modellers, the firm possesses a notable back catalogue of cars and commercial vehicles, some in very large scales, and has also produced a great number of aircraft kits. Many of the latter were made using other Japanese manufacturer's moulds – notably Imai and Kogure – and a great many were ex-Monogram (with whom Bandai had signed a co-operation agreement in 1976).

With many modellers, it has to be admitted that Bandai's high point was when it embraced the 'Patlabor' and 'Gundam' robot craze, producing dozens of these fantastic creations in a variety of scales and complexities.

Bandai introduced many modellers to the world of 'Gundam' in July 1980 with the advent of the classic

Contrast in styles, Bandai's amazing ⅟₈₅₀th scale USS Enterprise NCC-1701 from Star Trek and the tiny ⅟₄₈th scale 'Panzer IV' from 1973.

Gone but not forgotten, Bandai's classic ⅟₄₈th scale 'Pin Point' series.

Millions of Gundam owners can't be wrong.

DRAGON

Dragon ⅟₁₆th scale 'Warrior Series'. A figure modeller's dream.

President of Dragon Models Ltd (DML) Freddie Leung established the Hong Kong-based company in 1987 and created Dragon Shanghai as the company's mainland China operation prior to Britain returning Hong Kong to China when the 'lease' on the territory expired in 1997.

From the beginning DML designed and manufactured its own plastic model kits and exported them to all parts of the world via its agents in different countries. The high quality of DML products rapidly won the recognition of international modellers and the new company won many awards – notably from enthusiast magazines and modelling societies throughout the world.

DML constantly re-invests its capital, procuring the latest tools and equipment required to maintain such high standards. Since it began, DML has produced more than 600 items, a prolific rate of new releases not seen since the heyday of Airfix in the early 1970s.

Recently DML's products have also been marketed under the 'Revell/Monogram' banner in the USA, 'Revell' and 'Italeri' in Europe, and 'Hasegawa' and 'Gunze' in Japan.

When DML's ⅟₃₅th scale military vehicle and figure range first appeared in the late 1980s, the quality and variety of the new kits were the first serious challenge to Tamiya's iron grip on this sector for nearly 20 years. These kits often feature box-top illustrations created by respected military artist Ron Volstad, familiar to readers of *Military Modelling Magazine* and Osprey's classic *Men-At-Arms* range of enthusiasts' books.

In 1997, DML diversified into the airliner model field, manufacturing models for airline promotional use and for collectors. The resultant 'Dragon Wings' line of 1:400 scale aircraft has since grown to become one of DML's most successful and diverse series, representing unique liveries from nearly 100 commercial and government airlines. Maintaining strict standards to original aircraft specifications, working parts, accurate commercial markings and scale, Dragon Wings continues to hold a unique and respected position in the die-cast model aircraft industry.

The success of Dragon Wings encouraged DML to create an entirely new series of die-cast aircraft models – the 'Warbirds' – an ever-expanding line of 1:72 scale fighter aircraft ranging from WWII classics to the cutting-edge machines of today.

In 1999, DML diversified further, using all the skill and knowledge acquired with kits and die-casts to extend its modelling activities to the much larger 1/6 scale with the introduction of its 'New Generation Life Action Figure' series. As Dragon themselves say, "By the following January, this series – fully poseable military and licensed 12-inch figures featuring meticulously researched cloth uniforms, detailed weapons and equipment – was universally recognised as the new benchmark in high-quality collectable action figures, winning several awards from industry magazines and building a strong and passionate base of Dragon action figure collectors. The series currently stands at some 250-plus individual releases, with subjects varying from World War II, Modern Special Operations and Law Enforcement to licensed character figures from film, popular music, sports, electronic games and comics."

Buoyed by the success of its 1/6th scale figure range, DML has continued to expand its catalogue of figures aimed at collectors with a range of smaller items, the 'Dragon Minis' series of figures that are especially popular in Hong Kong and the 'Action18' series of ultra-realistic 1/18 scale fully poseable action figures. These figures, which Dragon claim feature "a unique composite of modelling and action figure philosophies", feature a comparable level of accuracy to Dragon's immensely popular 1/6 scale action figures, but are produced to a scale designed to appeal to modellers and diorama builders.

Currently, DML's wide-ranging business activities encompass everything from plastic model kits, action figures, die-cast collectables, to numerous resin, PVC and vinyl products.

Dragon's 1/35th scale military series range is superb.

EAGLEWALL

Eagle comic – what a brand!

The quiet Surrey town of Dorking seems an unlikely location for plastic kit manufacture, yet in the late 1950s its tiny West Street foundry was the birthplace of two classic brands.

After achieving some commercial success with a range of compact ⅟₉₆th scale WWII warplane kits, moulded in grey polystyrene and packaged in inexpensive polythene bags as Airfix had, and marketed under the foundry's 'Vulcan' brand name, its foundry set its sights on a potentially more lucrative commercial arrangement.

Publisher Hulton Press's *Eagle* comic, which had been launched in 1950 supported by a massive £30,000 advertising campaign, had become an institution with British schoolboys. Illustrated by the legendary Frank Hampson, *Eagle* is most famous today as the home of space pilot Dan Dare and his faithful sidekick Digby. The weekly comic chronicled the duo's struggle against the evil Mekon, one of the first of numerous malevolent space aliens, which have since become a staple of science fiction.

Along with its flagship sci-fi series, *Eagle* also served up popular stories of allied derring-do from the recent world war. The war was still a vivid memory for many readers and their families. *Eagle* featured regular stories, which looked at the famous battles, campaigns, and assorted weapons, which contributed to the war effort.

The Dorking Foundry decided that reissuing the existing Vulcan model kit range under the *Eagle* banner might revitalise their products. Consequently the range was repackaged in stout boxes emblazoned with *Eagle's* masthead and accompanied by full-colour illustrations in

Vulcan 'FW190' bagged, prior to rebranding.

Vulcan ⅟₉₆th 'Me109' boxed, prior to rebranding.

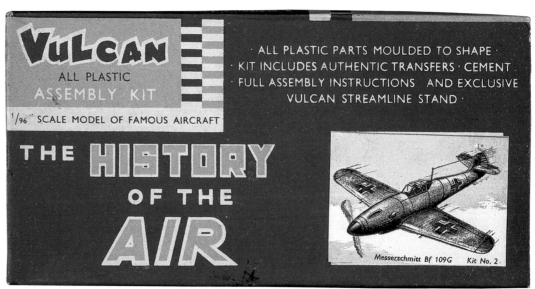

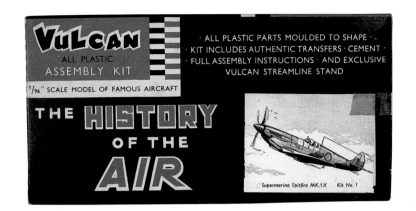

Vulcan boxed 'Spitfire'.

Classic Eaglewall 'Spitfire' – the same 'MKIX' version released by Vulcan prior to the deal with the publishers of *Eagle* comic.

Eaglewall *HMS Ajax*.

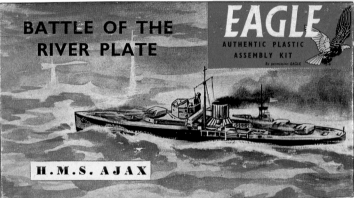

Eaglewall 'Battle of the River Plate' warship group.

Proprietor of 'Dorking Models', Anthony Lawrence, shows the author some of his large collection of Eaglewall classics.

Eagle's signature style (the bagged Vulcan range featured simple one-colour headers with dull illustrations, which doubled up as instruction leaflets). The new range was branded 'Eaglewall'.

Suitably born again, the 1/96th scale aircraft series was an immediate success with consumers and was soon supplemented with a range of WWII warships depicting incidents from famous naval battles. These included actions such as the 'Battle of the River Plate' and the famous *Altmark* incident, when British POWs were plucked from the eponymous German prison ship from the supposed security of a remote Norwegian fjord.

Enthusiasts will know that Eaglewall were adept at re-using supposedly identical sprues in an effort to release apparently identical sister ships like those in the Kriegsmarine's 'pocket' battle-ship class, for example. In reality the original ships differed considerably. This expedient enabled Eaglewall to rapidly increase their range at minimal expense!

Eaglewall produced models under license from other manufacturers. Notable amongst these were American

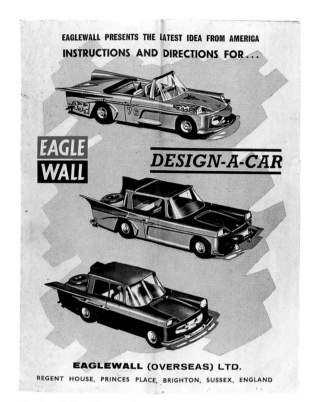

'Design-A-Car' instructions.

Eaglewall 'Design-A-Plane' packaging.

'Design-A-Plane' instructions.

manufacturer Pyro's 'antique' firearms and 'Design-A-Car' range. Despite such bold commercial initiatives, however, the firm ran into financial difficulties. Eaglewall was forced both to end its commercial relationship with Hulton's *Eagle Comic* and ultimately to cease all production in 1964. Consequently, Vulcan and Eaglewall kits are now sought-after collectors' items. For those keen to see how extensive the range is, I would recommend a visit to Anthony Lawrence's excellent shop, Dorking Models, where customers can examine probably the best display of such rarities in existence.

Eaglewall Royal Navy corvette and 'lend lease' US vessel.

Eaglewall Kreigsmarine auxiliaries.

Eaglewall ¹⁄₁₂₀₀th scale 'British Oil Tanker'.

Eaglewall *Altmark*.

Eaglewall *Tirpitz*.

Delightful (and very rare) Eaglewall 'U-38'.

HMS Prince of Wales battlegroup.

ESCI

1982 ESCI kit catalogue cover energetically illustrated by well-known Italian cartoonist Enzo Mario.

Italian company ESCI burst on to the international modelling scene in 1971 with the release of a stunning ⅛th scale replica of Germany's WWII 'BMW R-75' motorcycle/sidecar combination.

This huge model was so successful that it was soon joined by more ⅛th scale motorcycles: another German machine, a Zundapp 'Ks. 750', again with sidecar, a Moto Guzzi 'Alice' and an army Harley Davidson amongst them. The range even included a massive ⅛th scale replica of the Werhrmacht's 'Kettenkrad' motorcycle/half-track combination – one of the largest kits available.

Esci also produced a very nice range of ⅓₅th scale and ½nd scale military vehicles and in the early 1980s produced a range of aircraft, all 'DC-3 Dakota' derivatives, for the European market.

Famous toy firm ERTL purchased the ESCI moulds in 1987 and re-released many of the original kits under the ESCI/ERTL banner.

At the time of writing Revell-Monogram offer three of the best ESCI ⅛th scale originals: the BMW and Zundapp combinations, and, of particular interest because it has been unavailable for so long, the impressive 'Kettenkrad'.

The most collectible kits, however, are not surprisingly those in the original ESCI packaging dating from before 1987.

When first available in the mid-1970s, ESCI's range of massive ⅛th scale military vehicles and motorcycles were real head turners. This VW Kubelwagen was re-released shortly after the Ertl take-over in 1987. Today, Revell-Monogram are actively releasing many of Esci's earlier kits of ⅛th scale motorcycle and motorcycle/side-car combinations.

VW TYP 82 KUBELWAGEN
1/9th scale-maquette a monter 19"

FALLER

Most famous for their enormous range of polystyrene kits of buildings and other accessories for model railway layouts, the German firm of Faller has none the less developed an enviable reputation for providing some interesting models based on other themes – I have a pretty rare Faller ⅟₉₉th 'Ju 52 tri-motor' from the 1960s in my collection.

Established by brothers Edwin and Hermann Faller in 1946, originally as 'Hermann Faller' but soon changed to Gebr Faller. Once the Stuttgart-based pair returned to their Black Forest home of Gutenbach, Faller started operations manufacturing wooden combs. Aspiring to make wooden buildings for train layouts, sales of the range of combs secured some financial stability whilst the brothers organised the tools and equipment necessary for the precise manufacture of construction kits. Having scoured the local whereabouts for equipment which could be fashioned into tools – at one point even assembling a saw table from the remnants of a nearby aircraft wreck – the brothers unveiled their first true classic, the famous 'Marathon-Kit' which enabled buildings to be constructed to a modular pattern. To make ends meet, at the same time, Faller also produced a range of wooden games and household accessories such as coasters.

It wasn't until 1950 that Faller released their first true HO-OO scale models designed to partner accurately the model trains that were gradually re-appearing in war-torn Germany – most notably those of German company Marklin. During this period, the buildings were constructed from a combination of paper, glue and fine plaster – not plastic.

A major breakthrough at this time was Faller's development of their famous 'scatter material'. It was originally only available in green, but nevertheless this grass effect accessory proved invaluable to those wanting to achieve a scale effect on railway layouts. Originally Faller employed local schoolboys to mix the colorants with the finely ground saw chips comprising the mixture. Apparently, the 'Faller boys' stuck out at school by virtue of their green dyed forearms! Today dozen of colours and hues of this material are featured in Faller's catalogue together with their famous range of scale trees, built from similar materials adhering to mouldings of various tree species.

Faller began the production of polystyrene components to enhance their buildings in 1953. Initially these were confined to elements more suitable to the precision achievable from injection moulding, such as window frames, doors, chimneys, gutters and the like.

Faller's first real plastic construction kit – a model of a 'stone viaduct' first appeared in 1954. Amazingly this replica is still in Faller's range.

Faller's classic kit No. B-246 is still in the range. This example dates from 1958. I recall my father assembling a pair of these houses for my brother and me in 1972. They were to be added to our new railway layout. It took Dad ages to rub the supplied 'mortar' in between the tiny brick courses – but the result was well worth his effort!

At the Nuremberg Toy Fair in 1956, along with their growing range of railway accessories, Faller exhibited their 1/100th plastic aircraft range. They also unveiled a fully functioning miniature electric motor that could be incorporated in other manufacturers' scale models, enabling propellers to revolve with life-like effect.

A year later, the makers of the film 'Bridge over the River Kwai' commissioned Faller to make a scale replica of the famous bamboo bridge that supported Burma's notorious death railway. Suitably assembled, the model was presented to the film's star, William Holden.

In 1964 Faller introduced smaller 'N' gauge models, scaled to 1/160 for use by model railway enthusiasts with limited space for their layouts.

By the late 1960s, Faller's models were available worldwide and the firm's reputation for quality was

lectors like me, whose upstairs ceilings are also sagging under the weight of so much hoarded 'loft insulation', will reckon this prudence is perfectly acceptable. Mint and boxed kits hold their value!

In 1992 Faller put its toe into waters traditionally the domain of American manufacturers with the introduction of its 1/43rd scale 'Memory Cars' range, these being lavishly produced replicas of classic Mercedes-Benz cabriolets and coupés.

Faller celebrated its 50th anniversary in 1996. The following year it acquired the trademark and mould tools of competitor Pola and began to produce this company's 'HO' and 'N' gauge railway models.

At the time of writing Faller's 2003 catalogue weighs in at a hefty 420 pages featuring kits, mostly associated with railway layouts (the days of Faller's extensive aircraft range being long gone), but also includes a range of figures and accessories which will be popular with modellers in other areas.

Faller's exquisite 'Ju52' kit.

Military modellers, perhaps the main purchasers of this book, will be interested to learn of Faller's new 1/87th scale military programme, scaled as many enthusiasts will appreciate to the same size as the famous German ROCO 'minitank' range ('HO' scale). Along with Faller's ubiquitous buildings, this exciting range includes fine replicas of military barrack blocks, assault courses, sand-bagged emplacements, guard houses and vehicle sheds suitable for housing three miniature 'Leopard' tanks side by side. The series is complemented by a large range of 1/87th scale soldiers in a variety of poses and, perhaps most useful to military modellers, a selection of figures designed to be placed in the cupolas and drivers' hatches of tanks and armoured fighting vehicles.

firmly established. This reputation for excellence was further enhanced in 1984 with the introduction of Faller's 'Exclusive Models', a range of strictly limited-edition construction kits, the first of which 'Machine Factory' established the pattern of successive finely detailed replicas which came complete with a numbered certificate. Faller themselves say that "there are even collectors who buy these yearly appearing Exclusive Models only to put on their display shelf. The box probably never gets opened." I'm sure other kit col-

FROG

With £17,000 of share capital, in 1932 Charles and John Wilmot founded International Model Aircraft Ltd (IMA). Lancashire engineer Joseph Mansour quickly joined them. The brand name for IMA's products was 'FROG' and the honour of being the first manufacturer of scale model construction kits, entirely made from plastic, goes to them. Many will know that this curious brand name really relates to the period in the 1930s when the company produced delightful flying scale models. The firm claimed that each model **F**lies **R**ight **O**ff the **G**round!

Flying models such as the famous 'Interceptor' rode the wave of enthusiasm sweeping Britain at the time following the outright win in the Schneider Trophy seaplane race series in 1931. As the decade progressed and another war appeared imminent, Britain became 'air mad'. Aircraft, and aircraft models, drawings and storybooks with aviation themes were all the rage. IMA rode the crest of this unstoppable wave. Following the success of the ½nd scale mixed-media 'Skybirds' kits and with the introduction of new techniques of moulding new plastic acetates, IMA decided to manufacture a range of similarly scaled static model aircraft kits.

Consequently, FROG 'Penguins' (non-flying birds!), manufactured exclusively from cellulose acetate have the honour of being the first 'modern' plastic kits.

FROG Penguins first appeared in the shops during Christmas 1936. They were manufactured from cellulose acetate *butyrate,* one of the new thermoplastics that were

beginning to emerge from laboratories at the time. Cellulose acetate material possessed excellent moulding qualities and was far more stable than its sister material – the highly inflammable staple of the early film industry, cellulose nitrate. It was the numerous fires caused by cellulose nitrate stock that encouraged the photographic industry's urgent development of 'safety film'.

The first three Penguin kits were the 'Blackburn Shark MKII', 'Gloster Gladiator' and 'Hawker Fury'. They appeared in FROG's 1937/38 catalogue. Plastic model kits of a scale and type familiar to today's modellers date back to these first three Penguins. Despite wartime shortages, Penguins and Skybirds kits were manufactured throughout World War Two. The Penguin range increased substantially to include 'Spitfires', 'Hurricanes' and scale hangers, ambulances and anti-aircraft guns, encouraging the diorama builder to create whole airfields. There were even Penguin 'Dorniers' and

FROG advertisement (1930s).

Ultra-rare FROG Penguin 'Hawker Fury' (1930s).

FROG flying 'Spitfire' monoplane (1940s).

'Heinkels' by the time of the Battle of Britain in 1940.

Eventually the Penguin range was extended to include racing cars and maritime vessels such as tugs and destroyers. However, cellulose acetate, from which Penguins were moulded, was far from being an ideal material. It was difficult to sand and shape with a knife and could suffer from fatigue; resulting in warping and the emergence of a powdery chemical 'bloom'.

Penguin Plastic Racer.

FROG continued to support its enviable reputation with flying aircraft, even releasing minute petrol and diesel engines, which superseded their famous rubber band motors. By the early fifties their factories were manufacturing nearly 1,000 such engines every week.

Together with miniature combustion engines to further enhance their flying aircraft, IMA provided radio-control equipment. These sets weren't made at their own factory, but in part of Britain's famous Tri-ang Toys plant. Soon after IMA had been incorporated, Lines Brothers, owners of Tri-ang, had bought a controlling stake in the business.

FROG ½nd scale 'Spitfire II'.

Flying models were an important part of FROG's business but the firm never abandoned kit manufacture.

Although the famous Penguin range had disappeared from catalogues, in 1955 a new range of plastic kits was announced. This time the famous FROG brand was chosen for these new, all-polystyrene, kits.

At last competing with Airfix head-on, FROG suffered the disadvantage of breaking into the polystyrene kit market after the former had established market dominance. Because of FROG's smaller volumes, they couldn't negotiate the best discounts. Their margins were tighter and consequently their models sold for a higher retail price. Nevertheless, FROG kits were presented in packaging superior to the flimsy plastic bags their British rival had been forced to adopt in order to secure Woolworth's patronage.

The first FROG ½nd scale models represented some of Britain's recent breakthroughs in aviation technology, delta aircraft like Gloster's sleek 'Javelin' and English Electric's impressive twin-engine jet bomber the 'Canberra'.

A range of military vehicles and state-of-the-art air defence and multi-barrelled weapon systems (Bristol 'Bloodhound', Nike 'Hercules' and 'Ontos' light tank, etc), produced from mould tools leased by North American model manufacturer Renwal, soon complemented the aircraft range.

By the early 1960s, sales of FROG's flying models and engines were beginning to decline. Deals were done within the Tri-ang organisation and with Britain's A.A. Hales and America's Cox Corporation, to divest the company of too much involvement within a sector it no longer dominated.

FROG's plastic kit range expanded rapidly. Soon models of ships and cars were added to the catalogue. IMA's parent, Tri-ang, manufactured a successful model railway

range and it was decided that FROG's designers should also produce a range of HO scale model buildings and accessories for use on miniature layouts.

Always with an eye on packaging innovation – their patented one-piece box was a significant development – the company consistently enhanced the presentation of its kits. FROG's 'Trail Blazers' and 'Inside Story' kits were object lessons in design. The Inside Story kits came complete with an integral booklet that revealed the complexities and structure of the full-size aircraft replicated within. FROG even released models that came complete with moulded picture frames enabling the purchaser to cut out and display the exciting box top illustration. Their collectible Battle of Britain 'Combat Pack', for example, featured a ½nd scale 'Spitfire' and 'Ju 88' bomber which could be displayed fixed to a framed illustration of the two 1940 adversaries in combat. With the introduction of 'Spin-a-prop' motor-packs to enhance the propellers of ½nd scale kits, the great days of IMA's heritage were recalled.

In 1964 Tri-ang bought Meccano Ltd. Meccano had long enjoyed a presence and reputation in France, having a factory in Paris since 1921 and more recently a large production facility at Calais. In 1965 a FROG executive was encouraged to discuss closer links with French polystyrene kit manufacturer Heller, who had by then established a reputation as continental Europe's leading manufacturer. As mentioned elsewhere in this book, the kit industry being what it is, these facts would later have an ironic link to Airfix. Firstly, in the early eighties during the 'Palitoy years' Airfix kits were manufactured in the Calais Miro-Meccano factory which was owned by Humbrol. Airfix was twinned with Heller (also part

FROG ½nd scale 'Curtiss Kittyhawk'.

FROG ½nd scale 'Spitfire' and 'Ju88' complete with 'Exclusive picture frame display'.

FROG ½nd scale 'Lancaster' bomber.

Very collectible ½nd scale FROG 'Avro Shackleton'.

America's AMT kit company enabled FROG to further penetrate the somewhat protected North American market.

Despite releasing some large and eagerly awaited kits such as their now very rare Avro 'Shackleton' and delightful boxed 'Spitfire XIV and Flying Bomb' combination, by the end of the 1960s, FROG was still chasing the elusive 'pocket-money' brigade – schoolboy modellers. So, reluctantly the company cut the cost of its smaller models by emulating Airfix and ... putting them in a plastic bag!

As the 1970s dawned, the British toy industry was enduring a very difficult time. One of the casualties of this recession was Tri-ang, who were forced into receivership in 1971. Bought by rival toy giant Dunbee-Combex-Marx Ltd and with a number of FROG models in advanced production, the remnants of Tri-ang's kit interests continued under the 'Rovex' banner.

The early 1970s brought competition in the UK not only from Airfix, but also from Matchbox, well established in the die-cast toy vehicle business but a newcomer to plastic construction kits. Their, cheap, multi-coloured kits, which could be assembled to reveal a colourful replica without the need to pick up a paint brush, proved enormously popular with youngsters and particularly threatened FROG's less secure

of the Humbrol family), sharing the French kit manufacturer's production facilities in Normandy!

By the mid-1960s the sprawling Tri-ang group decided to shift FROG's production from Merton in South London to the factories of another subsidiary, Rovex Scale Models Ltd of Margate, Kent, it being decided that IMA and Rovex, both being model manufacturers, should share common operating practices.

By now FROG's kit range had expanded to more than 90 different models – which put great pressure on Rovex. The situation was eased by virtue of an agreement to share and repackage moulded parts with respected Japanese manufacturer Hasegawa. For FROG kits, Hasegawa were a way into the somewhat restricted Japanese market and Hasegawa's arrangement with

A real collector's item – FROG ½nd scale 'AW Whitley'.

FROG press ad in Gamages catalogue 1961.

FROG ¼₈th scale self-propelled 'Howitzer'.

FROG's earlier 'Spitfire MkII', repackaged as part of the exciting 'Inside Story' range.

FROG S.6B 'Trailblazer' in original box.

FROG ½₂nd scale 'Spitfire and Flying Bomb' – one of the firm's most successful kits.

81

market share. Airfix would simply have to produce even more new kits each month!

The final significant development in the FROG story relates to Dunbee-Combex-Marx's deal with the Soviet government during the mid-1970s. In order to secure lucrative trade agreements behind the iron curtain and hopefully obtain a slice of the huge Russian toy market - which the Kremlin had recently decreed should embark on a five-year modernisation plan which included the purchase of sophisticated toy-manufacturing processes and machinery from the west – DCM thought it might be a good idea to dangle the existing FROG tools as an incentive.

Consequently dozens of FROG's model tools – excluding any of Axis machinery – were shipped to DCM's Russian subsidiary NOVO. Mould tools, some which were so new they had not even appeared in FROG catalogues in the UK, continued to be sent to Russia at an alarming rate.

In 1977, when the tool-making and packaging of some great FROG kits, including 'Arado 234', 'Lancaster B Mk.1', 'B-17E' and 'Sea Vixen', had been completed, DCM decided to wind up the company. FROG packed and despatched its last moulds to Russia in November 1977.

An interesting postscript to the FROG story, as far as kit collectors are concerned, relates to the recent rise in

FROG Penguin Armstrong-Siddeley 'Hurricane' – on four wheels and without wings!

values of NOVO/FROG kits. Regarded with derision when they first appeared, the products of the now-defunct NOVO operation have, ironically, achieved a collectible status all of their own. Apart from enabling British modellers to reintroduce themselves to old FROG tools which they thought would never be seen again – the company's venerable 'Shackleton' and 'Whitley' spring to mind – NOVO kits have preserved a kind of pre-glasnost charm which many enthusiasts find endearing.

As far as FROG and Penguin kits are concerned, virtually any of the latter range is highly collectible, especially pre-war ones. Regarding 'Flying FROGs', the company's 'Interceptors' appear for sale with surprising regularity, testament to their enormous popularity over half a century ago. The really rare kits include FROG's 'Light Ship', 'Lifeboat', Vickers 'Valiant V' bomber, DeHavilland 'Comet' and Bristol 'Britannia' (both ⅟₉₆th scale and in RAF markings) and their classic replica of the 'R-100 Airship'.

I'm unsure of the precise whereabouts of much of FROG's tool bank. Some kits that originated in the FROG drawing offices turn up re-branded on the pages of the mainstream manufacturers. Some appear in the Far East. I suppose many still languish in Eastern Europe. Who knows when we might see some FROG classics again?

FUJIMI

Japanese manufacturer Fujimi originated in the early 1960s. Starting with a range of ⅟₇₀th scale aircraft models of mostly indigenous Japanese machines from WWII – 'Zeros', 'Tonys' and 'Franks', but also including some very collectable American machines, especially two marks of Chance-Vought 'Corsairs' – Fujimi's kit list has grown and grown.

Apparently, during its early days, Fujimi also released a range of ⅟₅₀th scale aircraft kits. As the company developed, it soon realised that both its ⅟₇₀th and ⅟₅₀th range were fractionally out of synch with ⅟₇₂nd and ⅟₄₈th, the two internationally accepted standards. So, without further ado, the company repackaged the kits and miraculously they fitted the two regular scales – without the need even to change the size of the moulded pieces inside!

Today, the Fujimi range is vast and extends to military aircraft, civil airliners, ships, vehicles and a notable range of military vehicles in scales ranging from ⅟₇₆th to ⅟₃₀th. Allegedly, many of the ⅟₇₆th line were acquired from Nitto in the mid-1980s.

In the late 1970s, Fujimi's AFVs were readily available in Britain and made a useful supplement to the similarly scaled military vehicles available from Airfix and Matchbox.

Fujimi ⅟₄₈th scale 'Spitfire V' (1970s)

Marvellous Fujimi 'British Tank Commander'.

HASEGAWA

Hasegawa can trace its origins back to the early 1960s. Today it ranks with Tamiya as one of the greatest kit companies in the world and is … Japanese to boot!

I understand that Hasegawa really entered the premier league of kit manufacturers following their purchase of a much smaller Japanese competitor, 'Mania', whose employees had demonstrated enormous proficiency in the kit design and tool-making field. This acquisition took place in the mid-1970s and certainly since around this time, Hasegawa's products have been second to none.

Apart from its curious range of 'Egg Craft' caricatures of famous aeroplanes, Hasegawa generally has a reputation for scrupulous accuracy, attention to detail and manufacturing finesse. The company has produced a vast range of kits of almost every subject and in all scales.

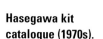

Hasegawa kit catalogue (1970s).

The company began with some ⅟₆₀th and ⅟₆₀th scaled gliders and a very desirable ½nd scale North American 'F-86F' issued in Blue Impulse livery in the 1960s. They then progressed to some truly massive ⅛th scale 'Museum Quality' WWI biplane fighters manufactured in wood, metal and plastic – Hasegawa has regularly demonstrated versatility and innovation. Indeed, the latter models are so good, I have often seen them in museums! Incidentally this impressive range spawned a series of separate models depicting each aircraft's power plant or machine-gun armament. I still have a complete 'SE.5A' in my collection, but I'm not sure I will ever be able to allocate the months and months needed to build it.

I understand that a very rare limited-edition model of a 'Disneyland Japan 747', manufactured for promotional use which dates from Hasegawa's earliest days, has become a Holy Grail for aircraft enthusiasts.

Military modellers revere Hasegawa as much as aircraft enthusiasts do. Indeed, at the time of writing Hasegawa has released an impressive ⅟₂₄th scale Willys 'MB Jeep' complete with driver, apparently engineered from an entirely new tool. No doubt all those looking for a suitable vehicle to accompany their 70mm figures will snap this up.

Their current range comprises aircraft from ½nd through ⅟₄₈th to ⅟₃₂nd scales and a selection of ½nd scale military vehicles or, for those with a maritime bent, some ⅟₇₀₀th scale waterline models.

HAWK

Beginning with a range of balsa wood flying models in the 1920s to satisfy a craze that was all the rage with youngsters worldwide, Hawk began to focus more on scale accuracy and very soon developed a range of plastic (John Burns thinks Bakelite) accessories which could be attached to their balsa flyers. All-plastic construction kits naturally followed. In fact Hawk are a candidate for the title of earliest North American plastic kit manufacturer – the plans in their ¼8th scale 'Curtiss R3C-1' are dated 1946. After an initially lukewarm reception it appears to have been a couple of years before toy or hobby shops stocked the actual kit. By the late 1940s, however, moulded in black, the little model had found an audience. Buoyed by the success of the 'Curtiss' replica and the models that followed it (including a ¼8th scale 'Gee Bee' racer and a very collectible ¹⁄₁₄₀th scale Lockheed 'Constellation' airliner), by 1951 Hawk had ceased manufacturing wooden flying models.

Hawk produced their first ½nd scale replicas in the mid-1950s. These actually started life as identification tools ('ID' models) destined for the US military, origi-

nally appearing as pre-assembled solid replicas. They were soon re-engineered and released as kits. Anyone fortunate enough to have a surviving example of a 'Hawk Supermarine Swift' from this period, either in kit or solid ID 'recognition' form, is sitting on a gold mine as far as British collectors are concerned.

Of all Hawk's kits, the most famous are arguably their fantastic range of 'Weird-Oh's'. As the name suggests, these kits were pure fantasy and featured an assortment of manic characters in a variety of activities that generally included components from a traditional and existing Hawk kit.

Rare Hawk 'Spirit of St.Louis' monoplane.

Hawk ¼8th scale 'OV-10A' reconnaissance plane.

HISTOREX

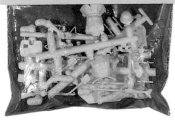

Unbelievably precise ⅟₃₅th Armour Accessories W.W.II German infantryman – in association with America's famous 'Squadron' brand.

Great days – as good as bagged kits ever got.

Modellers of my generation will remember opening the orange and white packets which contained Historex kits with fondness. For around 30 years this French manufacturer's range of 54mm Napoleonic soldiers set new standards for detail and accuracy. Historex's mouldings are still of unsurpassed quality. Towards the end of their reign the company released polystyrene miniature components of exquisite finesse. I remember their one-piece shakos or cornets with hollow bowls which seemingly defied the traditional restrictions inherent in 'under cutting' moulds. Historex appeared to produce the impossible.

It's probably no coincidence that the brand name 'Historex' sounds quite similar to 'Mokarex', because this French coffee brand was in fact key to the model manufacturers existence. Shortly after the Second-World War, the coffee supplier included 'free' premiums of miniature plastic soldiers with its popular ground coffee. These were based on the designs of Pierre-Albert Leroux and Lucien Rousselot, and tooled by master-engraver Jacques Fath. The resultant semi-round ('demi ronde bosse') polystyrene figures were enormously popular. Not surprisingly, a coffee brand that claimed its name was synonymous with 'quality' made great efforts to ensure that its 'Figurines

Historiques' series was also executed to the highest standard.

Variously scaled between 45 and 54mm, the Mokarex figures included foot and mounted subjects covering French military, royal and revolutionary subjects from the middle ages right up to the Great War. Soon the range had grown to over 400 figures, varying from a delightful 'Louis XI' period chess set (silver or gold plastic mouldings standing in for the traditional black and white pieces) which presumably required a lot of coffee drinking to collect, to my favourites, some 50mm mounted 'French 1914–18' troops released in 1959, each sculpted in the most naturally realistic poses imaginable.

However, over time, consumer tastes changed and eventually Mokarex became more associated with coffee makers rather than the ingredients of the drink itself. The figures ceased production. They had, however, proved so successful that in 1963, 'Atelier de Gravure' of Paris, the manufacturer of the premiums, decided to continue with model soldier production.

Under its 'Aeros' brand, the firm already produced plastic aeroplane kits, so, working with French artist and Napoleonic buff Eugene Leliepvre, they proceeded to produce their own 54mm model soldier kit. Branded 'Historex' the first release was a 40-part miniature of a French Revolutionary Wars 'Hussar'. It was warmly received and despite having no proper instruction leaflet and a length of paper tape that had to be cut to make belts and cross-straps, its manufacture established a pattern that was to continue for nearly 30 years.

Soon, Historex established an enormous range of foot and mounted figures all from the period of

Napoleon's 1st Empire. Early on they supplemented this range with exquisite replicas of period artillery, beginning with their '8pdr Gribeauval' field-piece in 1964. The field guns were also available with figures packaged in elaborate box sets. I well remember my father visiting London's 'Under Two Flags' and buying Historex's 'Friedland' artillery set for me. I ripped the shiny Cellophane from its stout crimson box at light speed!

One of the most significant developments in the Historex story was the establishment of Lyn Sangster's Historex Agents in 1967. Based in Dover, this distributor quickly forged an enduring bond with Historex. The British dimension also contributed to Historex's decision to expand its range to include soldiers from Napoleon's enemies and their allies and in 1970 Historex released the first of their famous 'Scots Greys' figures. The 'Scots Greys' were quickly followed by a series of 'Mamaluke Cavalry' that was received to huge critical acclaim when it first appeared in the shops.

In 1970, Historex Agents also published a stunning catalogue which, richly illustrated with wonderful colour photographs, introduced the work of master modellers Ray Lamb, Shep Paine and Pierre Conrad. An illustrated 'Spare Parts' catalogue that enabled modellers to pick and choose from Historex's enormous range of some 15,000 items accompanied this publication. Via their association with America's 'Squadron Shop' organisation, Historex agents also encouraged the Parisian firm to branch out into more modern figures with the release of the intricately detailed ⅟₃₅th 'Armour Accessories' range of WWII German soldiers and equipment.

In 1985 Historex Agents and Ray Lamb, who had now founded his seminal 'Poste Militaire' range of 75mm metal figures, established the annual 'Euro Militaire' event in Folkestone. This show became the forum for enthusiasts to see examples of the finest figure modelling, study the latest releases and meet their heroes.

Sadly, however, the gradual shift away from 19th- to 20th-century subjects and especially the huge growth in interest in WWII German armour, plus the burgeoning fashion in wartime dioramas, caused Historex's market share decline. Anyway, competition from other 54mm figures had intensified, especially with the appearance of a huge choice of Airfix's Napoleonic and W.II 'Multipose' range for example, and the rise of 'garage kit' short-run resin models. Apparently, all these developments conspired towards the decline of Historex.

By 1990 the Historex brand name had been sold and in 1991 the manufacturer ceased trading. Fortunately, all was not lost. The name survives and the independent Historex Agents continues to thrive.

In 1992 the new owners of the classic kit brand, Christian Sauve's company ADV, a manufacturer with an established reputation for excellent ⅟₃₅th scale figures and military vehicles, established NCO Historex. The abbreviation standing for 'Nouvelle Compagnie d'Origine', this new name enables a new generation of modellers to discover precisely why the name Historex is so revered.

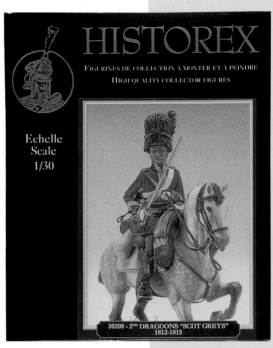

The great name lives on.

Nemrod figure by NCO Historex.

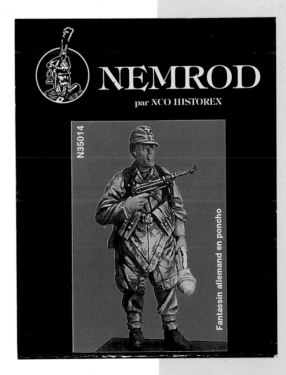

HELLER

Heller catalogue.

Heller has become better known to British modellers since partnering Airfix and Humbrol as part of the Hobby Products Group's business portfolio. Indeed, today all Airfix kits are manufactured at Heller's famous factory at Trun near Falaise in Normandy.

Although it shares the same initial capital letter as Gallic compatriots Historex, the firm of Heller predates the Parisian model soldier manufacturer and began trading in 1957. Its first kit was a ⅟₁₀₀th scale replica of the prototype 'Caravelle' airliner, naturally enough in Air France markings. This was an enormously popular model with Heller's home market and some time later was re-released, updated and with new registration codes. Heller also produced a smaller, ⅟₂₀₀th scale replica of Sud-Aviation's famous aircraft.

Heller's range is wide and varied, as one would expect from a 'traditional' manufacturer. Whilst their catalogue has always included a good number of French machines, especially aircraft, ships and military vehicles, they have regularly featured mouldings with a more international appeal. Like many manufacturers they have acquired tools from long-defunct manufacturers. Many of these, such as their ⅟₄₈th scale Supermarine 'Walrus' and ⅟₄₈th scale Fairey 'Swordfish' replicas, originated from British firm Merit.

Heller introduced their extensive ⅟₁₀₀th scale 'Cadet' range in 1963, enabling modellers to build a pretty comprehensive, but nonetheless compact range of then modern military aircraft – notably front line fighters and helicopters – and their early Sepecat 'Jaguars' and Sud-Aviation 'Gazelles' are very collectable.

In 1966 Heller's 'Sprint' series included the novelty of motors and working lights.

Despite a range which includes car models ranging from classics such as Citroen's classic '15 CV' in ⅟₂₄th scale to the Subaru 'Impreza WRC '02' in ⅟₄₃rd scale and

Heller kit from the 1990s.

Vintage Heller 'MiG21'.

which includes replicas of ESA's 'Arianne 5' rocket and even a ⅟₄₃rd scale Peterbilt 'Conventional Wrecker Truck' of 1980 vintage, I guess Heller is most famous for its wonderful models of fully rigged sailing ships.

With the release of fine replicas of the 'Soleil Royal' and 'HMS Victory' in massive ⅟₁₀₀th scale (still in the range) Heller really joined the front rank of kit manufacturers. With such a rich tool bank to call on, and over 45 years of model manufacture to call on, I'm sure Heller will continue to achieve consistently high standards, and, with Airfix, fly the flag for European kit manufacture.

Collectable Heller ⅟₇₂nd scale 'Bataille de France' set from 1990 – produced for the 50th anniversary of the Battle of Britain, or France, depending on which side of the Channel (or la Manche) you hail from!

Chasseurs Alpines

Assortment of Heller kits from the 1970s.

INPACT

This short-lived British manufacturer first came to note in the mid-1960s with the release of a range of ⅟₄₈th scale kits designed to capitalise on the success of the movie 'Those Magnificent Men In Their Flying Machines'. Inpact's range of aircraft in this series included a 'Bleriot XI', Bristol 'Boxkite' and 'Martin-Handasyde'.

Some of Inpact's other ⅟₄₈th scale model aircraft, like their Fairy 'Flycatcher', Bristol 'Bulldog' and Hawker 'Fury', later cropped up in Pyro, Lindberg or Life-Like branding.

Inpact Martin-Handasyde from 'Those Magnificent Men …'.

Those Magnificent Flying Machines

MARTIN-HANDASYDE

An authentic reproduction of the 1911 monoplane of the Antoinette type, which is featured in the 20th Century Fox film production "Those Magnificent Men in their Flying Machines" – or how I flew from London to Paris in 25 hours and 11 minutes.

INPACT KITS

Veteran Aircraft Series

Scaled from actual plans. Scale ¼"–1' complete with full assembly instructions and stand.

Inpact ⅟₄₈th scale 'Bristol Bulldog'.

INPACT KITS

BRISTOL BULLDOG

ADESTE COMITES

CLASSIC FIGHTER SERIES

32 Squadron RAF

ITALAEREI

Testors ½nd scale 'Spitfire Mk22'.

Perhaps because, other than for native Italians, this famous manufacturer's name was always a bit of a tongue twister, the company has now more or less adopted the easier pronunciation 'Italeri'.

Italians Gian Pietro Parmaggiani and Giuliano Malservisi began the company in the late 1960s, first trading as 'Aliplast'. The company went through some structural changes and re-emerged in 1971 with the current, or to be correct, more complex version of its well-known trademark.

Since then Italeri has established a reputation for moulding finesse and accuracy that few have managed to equal. Italeri kits of aircraft and military vehicles exhibit some of the most delicate mouldings available and the firm has a loyal fan base – notably in Britain – for the scale accuracy of its models.

From the early 1980s Italeri and American kit and hobby paint and accessories giant Testors began sharing mould tools. In 1990 Testors actually purchased the Italian company. Today, along with its extensive range of kits, Italeri's catalogue features Testor's ModelMaster range of enamel paints.

Happily, enthusiasts can purchase many Italeri classics. The firm's current catalogue runs to more than 100 pages and features kits of aircraft, motor vehicles, military figures and Italeri's respected range of diorama accessories. Amongst the many new models shown, enthusiasts will notice some old favourites like their

⅓₅th scale Opel 'Blitz' truck and 'Einheitskoffer' field command conversion and ½nd scale 'Waco' 'CG4' glider. Each of these kits, depicting machines from WWII, caused an enormous stir in the British modelling press when originally released in the mid-1970s.

⅓₅th scale Italaeri Jagdpanzer 38t 'Hetzer' from the mid-1970s – typical of the fine detail and first-rate moulding of this famous Italian manufacturer.

Italeri ⅓₅th scale 'US Rangers'.

JO-HAN

Famous North American model car manufacturer Jo-Han originates from the 1950s. The brand name is a contraction of 'John Haenle', the founder. Following a temporary pause in the early eighties the company was re-financed following an agreement with SeVille Enterprises and many rare and original car kits from Jo-Han's huge range soon reappeared.

Jo-Han ¹⁄₂₅th scale 'Turbine Car'.

Jo-Han's wonderful 'Heavenly Hearse'.

KLEEWARE

British company Kleeware is perhaps best known for being one of the first companies to engage in an enterprise which is commonplace with kit manufacturers today — namely sharing another's mould tool and re-branding a competitor's creation.

Along with an assortment of ships and vehicles, from 1956, Kleeware produced a variety of aircraft kits across the entire spectrum of scales. Get this: their model of America's famous Goodyear 'Blimp' came in ¹⁄₃₃₆th scale whilst their Stinson 'Trimotor' aircraft was moulded in ¹⁄₆₁st scale — two hardly very common ratios!

Comet Series Piper 'Apache' by Kleeware.

1960s kit assortment — the Kleeware US Navy 'Blimp' is especially collectable.

LIFE-LIKE

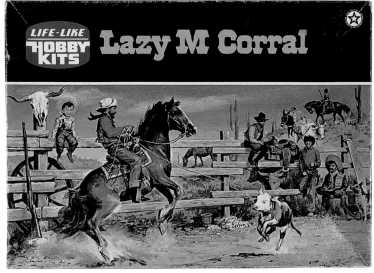

The 'Lazy M Corral'.

American predecessors like Adams, Pyro and Inpact originated many of the collectible kits from this US manufacturer. Consequently, these models, which date from the mid-1970s, include a real mixed bag of subjects.

In their patriotic 'American Wildlife' series, enthusiasts could opt for rather dull models of a Mallard Duck and Ring-Necked Pheasant or a spectacular Bald Eagle, wings vertical and claws outstretched as it prepares to strike its earthbound prey.

I have an elaborate 'Lazy M Corral' diorama in my collection, but despite searching high and low, I have never managed to trace surviving examples of Life-Like's ⅛th scale 'Cro-Magnon' or 'Neanderthal' figures. These models were first released in 1974 and show, respectively, our prehistoric ancestors, hunting or seated, surrounded by the impedimenta of such ancient daily life.

Following the success of films like 'Those Magnificent Men in their Flying Machines', everyone wanted a piece of the action.

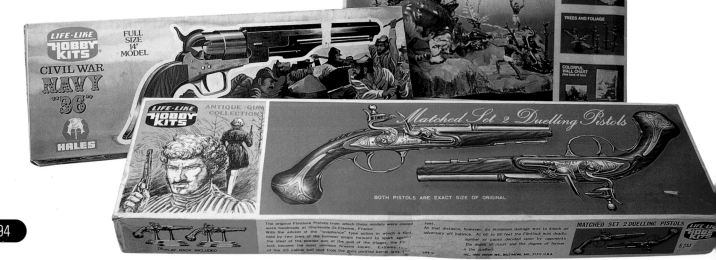

Life-Like kit assortment.

LINDBERG

Founded by Paul Lindberg in 1933, like many of its contemporaries this new company began its commercial activities by manufacturing balsa flying models. It wasn't until the late 1940s that his company, then trading as 'O-Lin', made polystyrene construction kits. These, a series of delightful ¼8th scale aircraft models of American machines, included Lockheed's 'Shooting Star' jet-fighter and North American's 'Sabre' – the aircraft which was soon to earn its laurels in Korea.

By 1950 the company adopted the more familiar 'Lindberg' brand and released a series of inexpensive models ranging from cars to ships and aircraft.

During the late 1950s Lindberg models were often sold under the 'Boycraft' brand. Many of the early O-Lin kits were repackaged this way, together with a very collectable 'Spitfire MkII' replica, in the usual American standard 'quarter-scale' (¼8th).

In his seminal *Plastic Aircraft Kits of the Twentieth Century and Beyond*, John Burns claims that Lindberg's 1996 re-release of a 1950s gift set, entitled 'Past-Present-Future' and including a pre-WWII 'Curtiss', a Douglas 'Stilleto' and a 'Flying Saucer', is a 'must have' for US collectors.

At the time of writing an interesting article by Tom Graham published in the March 2004 edition of *Fine Scale Modeler*, argues that Varney, a brand taken over by Lindberg's 'O-Lin' brand in 1951, might have claim to be North America's first polystyrene kit manufacturer, their 'PT boat', 'LST' and 'Fleet Submarine' kits apparently being available from early 1945!

Despite several 'brand evolutions' and consequent logo changes, and despite being taken over a couple of times since the late 1980s, Lindberg is still very much with us. Though never a manufacturer of the first order, Lindberg endures as one of those very few brand names that can trace its story back more than half a century.

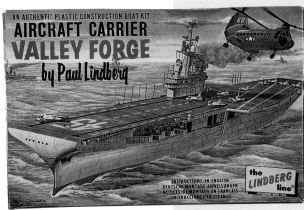

Rare model of America's 1950/60s period aircraft carrier – *USS Valley Forge*.

Lindberg's version of the famous 'Spitfire IX'.

Great box art!

MATCHBOX

The 'Matchbox' brand originates from 1947 when two unrelated friends, Londoners Leslie and Rodney Smith, started the business they had long dreamt of. Their new company was called Lesney Products, a name that combined syllables from each of their Christian names. Almost right from the start the pair were joined by engineering designer John ('Jack') Odell who quickly became Lesney's pattern and die maker and was made a full partner in the new business.

Lesney are most famous for their 'Matchbox' range of die-casts. Made of 'mazac', a robust zinc alloy, Matchbox toys were virtually indestructible. Their classic '1-75 Series' cars packaged in their striking – almost literally, because the yellow and blue design was based on a matchbox – yellow and blue boxes, sold by the

million. Today, mint and boxed examples from the early years of Lesney's production command a king's ransom at auction – but die casts are another story…

By the late 1960s, 'Matchbox' had become one of the biggest toy brands in the world. The company's products included cars of all sizes and Lesney also produced a range of toy motorways and accessories, examples of which could be found in almost every boy's bedroom.

Ironically, as the 1970 edition of the Matchbox die-cast catalogue speculated about future car design, it mused: "Plastic will be used increasingly for body shells…" Although speaking of car design, the company seemed to be considering plastic manufacture in a very uncharacteristic way. So, in 1971, the company took the decision to enter the very lucrative plastic construction kit business. By then the Matchbox brand was as well known as Airfix and FROG and the decision to compete in this vibrant sector made sound commercial sense.

Matchbox began its classic ½nd scale model aircraft series in 1973. The first in this initial range of ten models, PK-1 was a replica of the RAF's inter-war 'Hawker Fury' biplane. Fittingly, PK-2 was a 'banker', a model of a 'Spitfire MkIX'.

When they first appeared, these models, though crude by today's standards (remember the trench-like engraving on the panel lines?), caused a bit of a stir. They were cheap and because they came with separate sprues moulded in approximations of the finished machine's colours, they could be acceptably completed without the need

1980/81 Kit catalogue.

to resort to paint. Not surprisingly, it appealed to young boys, impatient to finish their pocket-money purchase. Matchbox kits caused quite a stir with their competitors. Airfix were forced to accelerate production of new releases, bludgeoning Matchbox who couldn't hope to compete with the South London manufacturer's variety and market presence. FROG, much smaller and always a relatively expensive brand, was given a nasty shock by the market acceptance of Matchbox's innovative approach in their sector.

Together with a growing range of ½nd scale aircraft, Matchbox added a creditable range of ⅙th scale military vehicles. Again, contrary to the practice of the growing range of Japanese manufacturers like Fujimi and Hasegawa who opted for the larger scale familiar to aircraft modellers, Matchbox chose the smaller scale adopted years before by Airfix and designed to complement HO/OO railway layouts. Matchbox military models had one major difference to the Airfix offerings. Each of Lesney's kits came complete with an easy-to-assemble scale diorama in which to display the model. Again, Matchbox strove to go one better than its direct competition. Matchbox designers were very imaginative in their choice of diorama settings. These ranged from shell-pocked, cobbled European streets to the sands of North Africa. Matchbox also produced a series of soft plastic ⅙th scale soldiers to complement their tanks and armoured vehicles and to directly challenge Airfix's long superiority in this cheap and popular field.

Not content with smaller models, Matchbox released some very large ½nd aircraft. Favourites of many others and mine were their RAF interwar Handley Page 'Heyford' and Supermarine 'Stranraer'. Very soon they ventured into the much larger scales of ½nd for cars and aircraft. Matchbox's releases of both a late war 'Spitfire' and post-war

DeHavilland 'Sea Venom' were welcomed, as they had long been on many a modeller's 'wants list'. Despite the somewhat heavy-handed detailing and their propensity for including multi-coloured parts, Matchbox regularly tackled subjects that had long been ignored.

In 1978 Lesney purchased most of American company AMT's tools and released many of these under the familiar brand name in the US and 'Matchbox' in the UK. In 1991, Odyssey Partners acquired Matchbox, adding it to its two other recent significant purchases – Revell and Monogram. Since then, many of Matchbox's earlier military models have reappeared in themed combinations of vehicles and soldiers.

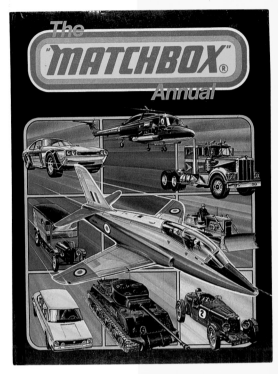

So confident, they even supported their kit and toy range with an annual.

Matchbox classics from the late 1970s.

MONOGRAM

Pooling their combined life savings of $5,000 Robert Reder and Jack Besser founded Monogram in December 1945.

As a youngster 'Bob' Reder was a very keen aero modeller who made flying model aircraft constructed from balsa wood and covered with doped tissue. These were powered by twisted rubber bands that, as they unwound, spun miniature propellers fast enough to pull the lightweight models skyward. He joined the local aero club and regularly flew his creations in the fields surrounding his Chicago home. After high school Reder joined the staff of The Comet Model Airplane Company where he had previously worked part time on Saturdays.

The advent of war meant that balsa wood, which originated from Ecuador, was in short supply. In America, imported balsa was requisitioned by the military for the construction of floats. Across the Atlantic, the British used this lightweight material as a component of the laminate construction of de Havilland's 'Wooden Wonder'; the twin-engined 'Mosquito' fighter-bomber.

Adopting more readily available basswood, Comet switched production from flying scale models to recognition models which were then the easiest way for pilots, air-gunners and civil defence personnel to familiarise themselves with the silhouettes of enemy aircraft. Interestingly, Comet also made 'Target Kites',

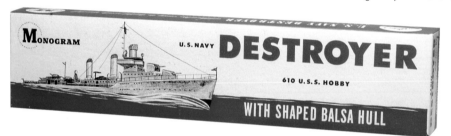

November 1945 and Monogram's first kits are released. Among them are the destroyer *USS Hobby* and the aircraft carrier *USS Shangri-La*. Each wooden model came with a shaped wooden hull.

Cessna '180 Sport' plane complete with detailed engine.

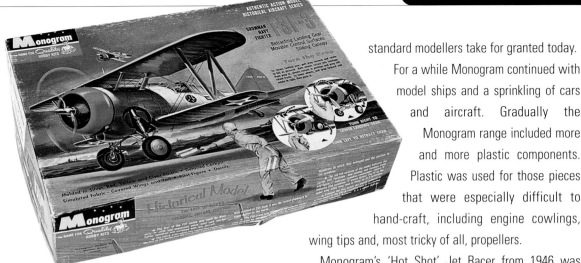

Top marks to the kit designer – just look what happens when you turn the prop.

standard modellers take for granted today.

For a while Monogram continued with model ships and a sprinkling of cars and aircraft. Gradually the Monogram range included more and more plastic components. Plastic was used for those pieces that were especially difficult to hand-craft, including engine cowlings, wing tips and, most tricky of all, propellers.

Monogram's 'Hot Shot' Jet Racer from 1946 was typical of the firm's construction style at the time. Consisting of a partly shaped wooden body, sheet balsa wood components and rubber wheels, it required hours of careful shaping and not inconsider-

large diamond-shaped kites with the silhouettes of Japanese fighters painted on them, hoisted skywards for gunnery practice.

Whilst at Comet, Reder met Jack Besser, the company's sales manager. Soon, the two colleagues began thinking about the opportunities an end to wartime hostilities might bring.

They concluded that the best plan was to form their own model company and at the war's end they established 'Monogram' in Chicago, Illinois.

As early as November 1945 their first three kits were released for sale. These true classics were a 'Landing Ship Tank' (LST), the destroyer *USS Hobby* and, appropriately, the cruiser *USS Chicago*. Each wooden model came with a 'shaped wooden hull' but required a great deal of extra labour to finish them to anywhere near the

¹⁄₃₂nd scale 'Blue Thunder' helicopter.

'Space Taxi' and contents.

Monogram Refueling Group duo.

¼th scale 'Hot Shot Racer' from 1967.

ing rather more precision-engineered moulded plastic components, which really paved the way for the company's future success in plastic construction kit manufacture. In 1952 Monogram's 'Super Kit' range finally put paid to the tiresome shaping required to realise accurate fuselage contours – 'Super Kits' came complete with perfectly preformed wooden parts.

Inevitably it wasn't long before Monogram abandoned wooden parts altogether. In 1954 the company released its first entirely synthetic model kit, the famous All Plastic Scale Model 'P-1 Midget Racer'. A 1932 Ford 'Roadster' and the 'Dipsy Doodle' speedboat immediately followed this. In their original packaging this trio of kits is highly sought after.

In 1957 Monogram's famous 'Snark Missile' appeared. Together with the aforementioned cars and aircraft, this example of space-age technology set the seal for the three types of model for which Monogram is now perhaps most famous.

able patience, before the streamlined vehicle on the box top could ever be realised. It did, however, feature an injection moulded transparent canopy!

It was, though, Monogram's famous 'Speedee-Bilt' flying model aircraft, incorporat-

In 1960, Monogram began to develop their famous ¼8th scale or 'quarter scale' range of warplanes. At the time this went against the grain in the United States as modellers had happily adopted the far smaller ½nd scale, which had originated in England in the 1930s.

Revell-Monogram's late, great facility at Morten Grove, a suburb of Chicago.

Monogram's decision to adopt ⅛th scale was prescient. Very quickly American modellers embraced this as the norm for model kits and today even in Europe ⅛th has fast replaced ½nd.

After enjoying significant commercial success, in 1961 Monogram moved to a purpose-built 120,000 square feet plant at Morten Grove, a suburb northwest of Chicago.

In those days, like Revell, Monogram held up a mirror to US achievement, producing kits, which reflected the myriad inventions charting the nation's scientific progress. Whilst Revell had initially focused on the existing products of America's revolutionary motor industry, after the introduction of its 'Hot Shot Racer', Monogram had long focused on the future.

Of all these areas of technological development it was the fields of ballistic missiles and space exploration which generated most subject matter. Fuelled by the urgent technological advances triggered by the Soviet Union's astonishing achievements following the launch of Sputnik in 1957, there was now an abundant supply of new and projected American rocket and spaceship developments for Monogram to model.

Monogram quickly released replicas of America's contributions to the 'space-race' and the manufacturer marked all of NASA's milestone inventions through the 'Gemini', 'Mercury' and 'Apollo' programmes. The company also immortalised many of the weird and wonderful hypothetical designs that abounded at the time, committing them to polystyrene kit form.

At the war's end, most of Germany's WWII 'V-weapon' rocket engineers were spirited away by American intelligence to work for the US Military. The most famous of these individuals was 'V2' designer Werner Von Braun. However, a colleague of his, Willy Ley, was probably a more prolific, if fanciful, visionary. Monogram's extensive range of Willy Ley 'Signature Designs' depict many of his weird and wonderful proposals and have since become enormously collectible.

In 1968 Monogram was incorporated into Mattel Inc, the world's largest toy company and owner of 'Barbie' and the ever-popular 'Hot Wheels' range of die-cast cars.

In 1970 Monogram established the 'Snap Tite' range of kits. Requiring no gluing, these kits were particularly easy to assemble and consequently very popular with novices. It wasn't long before most of

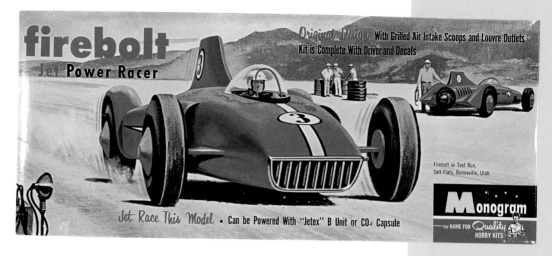

Monogram reissue of a 1950s classic, but where can you buy 'Jetex B units' these days?

Popular in the late 1950s and much sought after now, Monogram's 'Phantom Mustang' took kit manufacturing to new heights.

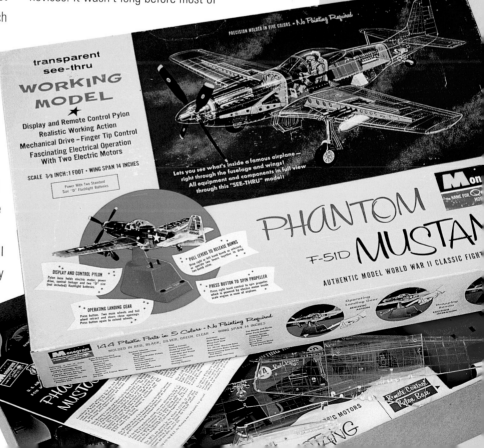

Monogram's Masters of the Universe 'Talon Fighter' and 'Attak Trak' from 1979.

Monogram's competitors released their own ranges of similar easy to assemble models. The Airfix range was called 'Snap Fix'!

In 1977 Monogram bought famous American kit manufacturer Aurora. Shortly after the deal had been completed many of Aurora's precious steel mould tools were badly damaged in a rail freight accident whilst *en route* to Morten Grove. Two years later, the ever-growing company opened up another facility, this time in Des Plaines.

In January 1984, Tom Gannon, Monogram's new Chairman, led a management buy-out, which purchased the company from Mattel. For two years, life at Monogram continued at a steady pace with the company introducing a new range of ⅛th scale cars and introducing the brand new ½th scale '57 Chevy' to all-round acclaim.

In 1986, it was New York company Odyssey's turn to buy Monogram; they also secured an option to buy Revell. Exercising this soon after, they decided to merge the company with Revell to complete their purchases in the plastic kit business. Revell's mould and equipment

Willy Ley's legendary 'TV Orbiter'.

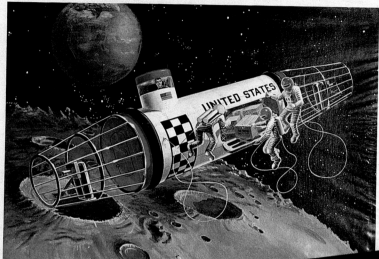

'Space Buggy' looking surprisingly similar to Willy Ley's 'Space Taxi' but … where's Willy?

was moved from its famous Venice, California facility to Monogram's Morten Grove HQ and so-called 'Plant II' at Des Plaines. Revell, Inc. was to be the parent company with Monogram its subsidiary.

Following the 1990 floatation of Revell AG in Bunde, West Germany, in July 1991 Revell-Monogram went public. In 1993 Revell-Monogram were merged into one company. However, all wasn't quiet for too long because in December 1994 Hallmark/Binney & Smith purchased them.

So, Revell-Monogram began the new year of 1995 as a wholly owned subsidiary of Binney & Smith, most famous as the owners of the 'Crayola' brand.

'The NAM Tour of Duty' TV series gives Monogram's ¹/₄₈th scale 'Skyraider' a new lease of life.

Kits of short-lived TV series quickly become collectable.

In September 2001, following five years of relative calm, Iowa-based Alpha International, best known for its 'Gearbox' brand of die-cast collectables and also the owner of Empire Stores, manufacturers of America's famous 'Buddy-L' and 'Big Wheel' brands, announced that now it had acquired Revell-Monogram. "We see the acquisition of Revell-Monogram and Revell AG as a strong complement to the existing Alpha structure," said Jody Keener, Director of Marketing and Production for Alpha International. "Jim Foster will remain as President and we see enormous potential from cross-selling product lines between Gearbox, Empire, Revell-Monogram and Revell AG. We also see opportunities to leverage our combined design, marketing and new product capabilities while increasing plant production capabilities in our Morton Grove facility," he added.

On 15 November 2002 RM Investments acquired Revell-Monogram and also Revell AG in Germany. They also established Revell-Monogram Asia Pacific with an office in Hong Kong to, as Chicago-based RM Investments' Chairman and CEO John Long said, "manage the development of distribution into areas not yet covered." Long also said plans were well under way to develop new product lines and further develop current ones "in order to further enhance Revell-Monogram's brand equity." Clearly model enthusiasts and especially those who, like me, adore Revell and Monogram's classic kits, can look forward to a very bright future.

A short post-script: Late in 2003, shortly after I visited Revell-Monogram's facility at Morten Grove and was able to study closely kit production, packaging and marketing (kindly arranged by the company's Ed Sexton), I learned that there had been another move. This time Revell-Monogram wasn't travelling far. Indeed the move to 725 Landwehr St. Northbrook is a number of blocks closer to Ed's home. So, I guess he has time for an extra cup of coffee before he leaves for work in the morning!

Joint promotion with Universal and the film 'Backdraft'.

Gimmick. What gimmick?

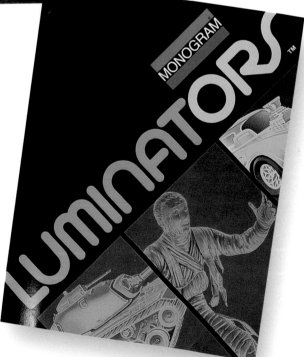

Revell-Monogram's genial Ed Sexton outside his home, holding an ultra-rare 'Midget Racer'.

Bill Lastovich, Product Planning Manager, Revell-Monogram, selecting an early Ed Roth car kit from the hundreds of rarities in Revell-Monogram's archive.

Hundreds of classic Revell-Monogram mould ('mold') tools in store at Morten Grove.

Injection-moulding machine at Revel-Monogram's Morten Grove facility. Note the hopper feed and the massive hydraulic ram, capable of exacting tons of pressure on the enclosed tool.

NITTO

Nitto began life in Japan in 1962. Since then, this energetic company has produced a vast range of models of all types in a variety of scales. In the 1970s Nitto issued a model of a 'Gemini' astronaut charmingly classified as a 'Space Pilot'!

Military model makers welcomed its vast range of relatively inexpensive 1/76th and 1/35th scale tanks and AFVs, and its enormous range of model aircraft, ranging from a 1/600th scale 'Concorde' in JAL markings to a far larger 1/32 scale Japanese Yokosuka 'K5Y2 Willow' floatplane, are coveted by kit collectors. Many of Nitto's 1/100th scale airliner tools were acquired and re-issued by Japanese manufacturer Doyusha.

However, for me and many other enthusiasts the most sought-after Nitto originals belong to their short-lived 'SF3D' science fiction range.

SF3D was collaboration between the artist and model maker Kow Yokoyama, the writer Hiroshi Ichimura and the graphic designer Kunitaka Imai. The trio were greatly aided in their endeavours by the patronage of *Hobby Japan* the high-quality Japanese model magazine with a leaning towards science fiction and fantasy.

The pages of *Hobby Japan* gave birth to a unique experiment, a comic book style story series illustrated not with pen and ink drawings but photos of model miniatures. The stories followed the battles between colonists resettling a nuclear-devastated planet Earth and the incumbent military government – the so-called 'Shutoral Demokratische Republik'.

The combatants

Nitto 1/35th scale 'Sdkfz251/1' (1970s).

wore retro-styled faintly Germanic uniforms of 1939–45 vintage and did battle in a vast array of armoured suits, robot landers and armoured crawlers, each sprouting an assortment of weaponry which ranged from heavy-calibre machine guns to Nazi 'Panzerfaust' bazookas last carried by German soldiers defending the ruins of Berlin!

The various 'Maschinen Krieger' vehicles designed by Yokoyama, Ichimura and Imai had equally pastiche Wehrmacht names such as 'Neuspotter', 'Fledermaus' and 'Hornisse'.

Scaled to a very manageable ⅟₂₀th, these kits are very finely moulded and for my money are the best science fiction kits available. Nitto had thought carefully about every aspect of the presentation of these models – the boxes themselves were printed on buff-coloured board with subtle rust colours. Each looked very 'official' and came with a colour photo of a superbly assembled kit affixed to the box top for use as a colour guide.

The 'Patlabor' and 'Gundam' craze very quickly eclipsed SF3D. This robot fighting machine fantasy swept Japan and the vast range of associated models, primarily by Bandai, were soon far more popular with consumers.

SF3D has its own distinct cadre of enthusiast, however, and today it is enjoying a resurgence of interest. Indeed, many of Nitto's original designs have re-appeared following an agreement with manufacturer 'Model Kasten' who are re-issuing some of the kits as limited-edition resin and plastic hybrids.

Nitto ended regular kit production in 1985. Doyusha acquired many of the moulds and re-issued several of the ⅟₁₀₀ airliner kits in the late 1980s and early 1990s. Some ex-Nitto kits were still available as of late 2002. Although kits have appeared with the Nitto logo in recent years, these are primarily for the Japanese market and are based on science fiction subjects from movies and TV programmes.

S.F.3.D. assortment.

PYRO

Originating from the early 1950s until 1972 when it was acquired first by US kit manufacturer Life-Like and then by Lindberg, Pyro produced a real variety of different kits.

Amongst an extensive range of kits of aircraft, ships and especially cars and motorcycles, the company is probably most famous for its ⅛ scale (life-size) series of antique weapons. This series included large replicas of rifles like Pyro's classic 'Moorish Rifle' and 'Western Saddle Rifle' and side arms which included revolvers like a 'Western .44' and 'Civil War Navy .36' to an extensive range of older flintlocks and wheel locks.

When you consider the limitations of the injection-moulded polystyrene process, the fact that Pyro's 'Kentucky Rifle' was nearly four-and-a-half feet long is simply amazing. What's more, each replica came complete with a handy wall rack, enabling modellers to display their purchases in a most effective way.

From 1962, some of Pyro's replica weapons were produced under licence in the UK by Eaglewall (who also released some of Pyro's equally memorable 'Design-A ...' range).

Pyro 1915 vintage 'Ford Pie Wagon'.

Pyro French 'Wheel Lock pistol'.

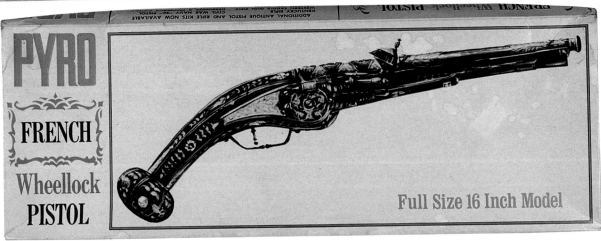

RENWAL

The revolutionary 'Aero-Skin'.

1957 Vintage catalogue.

Though well known to modellers worldwide, New York's Renwal Toy Corporation was never a 'purist' kit manufacturer. Indeed, despite including kits of both a Martin 'Mars' and Boeing 'B-17' bomber in a toy compendium dating back to the late 1940s until the mid-1960s Renwal's catalogues were full of toys.

The only vaguely accurate aircraft miniatures in Renwal's 1956 catalogue are replicas of America's 'Panther' and 'Thunderstreak' jets – available in 'unbreakable polyethylene'. Even simpler were the bagged '3 Piece Plane' sets ("to hang on a rack … to sell from a counter") of which retailers could purchase four bags ("12 planes!") for the very reasonable sum of $6.00. However, what would current toy collectors pay for Product No. 273, an elaborate toy diorama of the 'Panama Canal' which filled with water and had working locks representing the entrance and egress of the Atlantic and Pacific oceans? The 'Renwal TV Mobile', "a new type of toy designed for the young technician to practice field telecasting of the big sports event, parade or news story…" is my favourite from the same catalogue.

Despite subsequent toy catalogues featuring wonderful products (to us military modellers) like Product No. 309 'Military Set' which included a jeep, ambulance, guided missile, armoured car, tank, howitzer with … 'cut-out soldiers', it wasn't until the 1960s that Renwal entered the construction kit business proper.

Beginning with a selection of educational models that revealed the internal anatomy of humans ('Visible Man' & 'Visible Woman'), Renwal produced an extensive range of 'see-though' replicas of objects as diverse as the human eye and the anatomy of a cow. However, the firm is best known amongst modellers for its intricate

aircraft models that caused quite a stir when they first appeared.

In 1966 Renwal released the first of their famous 'Aero Skin' kits. These two model sets, entitled 'Fabulous Flying Machines', featured ½nd scale replicas of some of the earliest flying machines ever built. Not surprisingly, one of them was the 1903 'Wright Flyer' that was twinned with 'Bleriot's 1909 monoplane'. The extensive range also included a Curtiss 'Golden Flyer', an Avro 'Triplane', an 'Antoinette monoplane' and a Voisin 'Farman' biplane. All these were kits for which modellers had long waited.

The most remarkable component of these kits, however, was the inclusion of 'A Renwal Exclusive' called 'Aero Skin'. This consisted of delicate tissue paper, which had to be carefully cut and affixed to the wings and fuselage, moulded to represent only the skeletal framework of each aircraft's construction. Although the tissue was to be glued in place with the Testor's liquid cement supplied, the fact that the frameworks of each aircraft were moulded in black, rather than more accurate brown polystyrene, didn't really encourage scale realism.

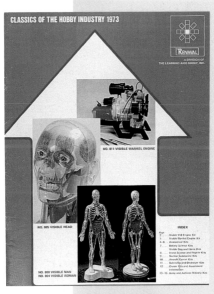

Renwal – 1973.

Despite the fact that the kits were clearly marketed to capitalise on the success of the new cinema release, 'Those Magnificent Men In Their Flying Machines', around which, incidentally, British firm 'Inpact' had produced a range of ¹⁄₄₈th scale models based on the machines featured in the film and which they proudly exhibited at Brighton's 1966 Toy Fair, sales of Renwal's models were very poor.

Consequently, Renwal abandoned the very complex aircraft from the first generation of flight and released some simpler 'Aero Skin' clad machines dating from WWI. Amongst these were ¹⁄₃₂nd scale and ¹⁄₄₈th scale models including Camels, Spads, Nieuports and Fokkers.

By the mid-1970s Renwal had ceased trading and in 1979 US model giant Revell (now Revell-Monogram) acquired many old Renwal tools. If we will ever see any of Renwal's famous 'Aero Skin' range again is up to them. If the kits do reappear though, I'm not sure collectors will be too happy. Some of the earliest Renwal kits command premium prices!

What would the Valient (sic) kit command on the second-hand market today?

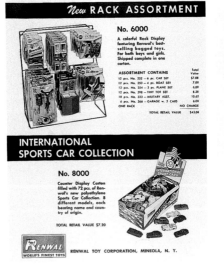

Far left: **1950s Dealer incentive.**

Left : **1956 Catalogue.**

REVELL

Revell and Monogram are to America what Airfix and FROG are to the United Kingdom – household brands synonymous with model kits and one of youngsters' stepping-stones to adulthood.

Prior to their merger, Revell and Monogram were independently famous the world over. Revell can date its genesis to 1943.

Like Airfix, Revell really entered the construction kit business by accident. It was founded by Lew Glaser, who had previously set his heart on a radio sales and repair business in Hollywood. Unfortunately for Lew, the exigencies of America's war effort forced his wireless venture out of business – the supply of new valves and electronic components being prioritised for the exclusive use of the military. So, before the war's end, Lew was forced to look for new opportunities.

Revell can trace its origins to Precision Specialities Inc., a plastic injection-moulding business that Lew invested in following the demise of his earlier enterprise. The company's first really successful product was a ladies' compact mirror; the firm's brand name, Revell, sounded a bit like cosmetic giant 'Revlon' which Lew thought quite appropriate. Revell produced myriad inexpensive domestic items, such as picture frames and cigarette cases, demonstrating the practical qualities of plastic moulding throughout. Despite some success, however, Lew Glaser was forced to supplement Precision Specialities' income by accepting occasional contract jobs for the armed forces switching injection-moulding capacity to the temporary fabrication of plastic components that were to be increasingly found in naval vessels and warplanes.

During the remainder of the 1940s following the advent of peace, Revell continued to manufacture toys and novelties which included collectible gems like the 'Toy Radar Radio' or the 'Toy Washing Machine', which claimed 'washes and wrings dolly's clothes'.

Although construction kits hadn't yet become a feature of Revell's catalogue the giant leap forward was around the corner. How it happened really echoes Airfix's entry into the kit business and, like the British firm, it was all down to a model vehicle!

In 1949 Revell was granted a licence to manufacture some of the toys designed by British ex-pat Jack Gowland. He was a former WWI balloon corps observer and had moved to California with his family shortly after the end of the Second World War.

Revell 1962/63 catalogue. '3d' in 'old' money – equivalent to a bargain one and a quarter New Pence today!

Gowland Highway Pioneers 1951/52.

Highway Pioneers – 'The Gowland Connection', 1951/52.

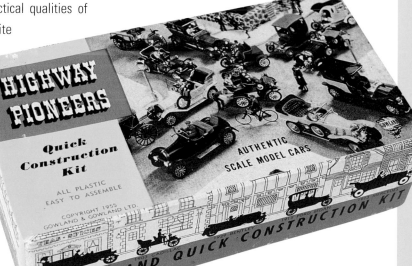

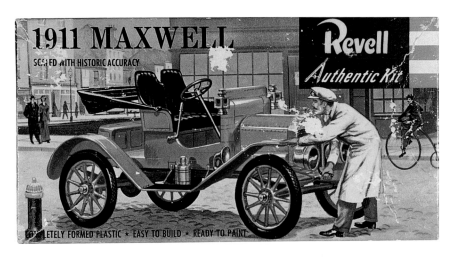

**Revell's famous
911 'Maxwell'.**

pioneers series' of kits was born. Without realising it, Revell's future success was assured.

The huge success of the 1911 Maxwell encouraged Revell to produce a sister model, a similarly scaled 'Back Firing Model-T Ford'. It also featured a pull cable; this time equipped with a trigger, which fired a hidden cap-gun mechanism – *voila* a backfire!

Although the pull-cord models, rather closer to toys than scale replicas´, of course, were successful, it was the demand for the smaller ⅟₃₂nd scale 'Highway Pioneer' construction kits which encouraged Glaser to focus entirely on precision scale replicas. Goodbye to toys (by now surplus supplies of the ladies' compact had been sold to Mattel who found it an ideal accompaniment to dolls' accessories).

By July 1952 Revell, well into production of a second series of five additional 'Highway Pioneers', established a dealer promotion that heralded the 'car of the month' and encouraged retailers to purchase new models on a monthly basis.

Gowland's company also designed a range of ⅟₃₂nd scale cars which were marketed either as assembled 'pull-cord' toys, or available in parts, as construction kits.

A chance meeting at a trade show in New York with toy and hobby distributor Sol Kramer led to an enormous order for one of Gowland's designs (a ⅟₁₆th scale 1911 Maxwell auto) and encouraged Revell to extend its model car range. The famous Revell/Gowland 'Highway

The enormous success of Revell's car kits didn't go unnoticed by competitors. By the mid-1950s many potential rivals invested in polystyrene injection-moulding technology and regardless of imports from Britain's FROG and Airfix, California-based Revell's market share was being threatened by US manufacturers such as New York companies Aurora and Premier Plastics. Further afield, Chicago's Monogram was also proving a significant competitor.

Consequently Revell was encouraged to extend its range to include subjects from every sector. However, this had the happy result that by the late 'fifties Revell had once again achieved market supremacy. Now it was offering scale replicas of cars, aircraft, military vehicles, ships and, notably, models relating to

America's new frontier, the conquest of space.

By 1960 Revell's catalogue included perennially popular classics like the 'Robert E. Lee' riverboat, Boeing 'B-52 'Giant' Stratofortress', 'Flying Dragon' 'B-25', Douglas 'Skyrocket' and Sikorsky 'H-19' helicopter (which endured well into the 1980s). These ever-popular models were accompanied by rather more exotic and consequently far more collectible miniatures of US air defence missiles. These included the Northrop 'Snark', Bendix's 'Talos' and an elaborate diorama which featured Convair's 'IBM'. Scarcer-than-hen's-teeth replicas from the period include the Westinghouse sponsored 'Atomic Power Station' and a number of ½nd scale vignette gift sets featuring rival combatants from the Battle of Britain and subsequent Battle of Berlin. Revell even produced a range of cardboard 'Revell-O-Ramas' that provided ready-made dioramic settings in which to display their ½nd scale aircraft models.

However, I guess if there is one salient difference between British and American model kit tastes it is each market's demand for either automobiles or scale aircraft. Aviation modelling is a much smaller fraction of the hobby in America and, vise versa, car models have marginally less appeal to British modellers.

One type of model auto with international appeal with which Revell will be forever connected is the hot rod or dragster. These models date back to the 1950s when many customised 'funny cars' sprang from the beat generation. Lots more emerged during the early 'sixties and later 'flowered' during the summer of love.

One name of car designer above all others is inextricably linked with Revell: that of the late 'Big Daddy', Ed Roth.

Born in 1932, Ed Roth was the artistic son of an immigrant German cabinetmaker who, after a brief spell with the US Air Force, applied his more creative talents to the

Don Garlits' 'Dragster', 1974, 'JU88', 1975 and 'M56 SP Gun', 1958.

Bell's famous 'X-15' record breaker – a Revell kit dating from 1959, 'Martin Seamaster', 1956, 'Douglas Stiletto', 1957 and 'Phantom F4K', 1968.

art of 'striping'. This is an auto-painting technique from the 1930s, which was enjoying resurgence amongst California's hot rodders. He also applied his, not inconsiderable, mechanical talents to the art of customising and converting the many jalopies that the newly affluent American youth was buying and 'chopping' with abandon. Soon, in partnership with Bud 'The Baron' Crozier, a veteran of the original striping and hand lettering industry and Crozier's grandson Tom Kelly, the trio established their Californian business, 'The Crazy Painters'.

By the early 1960s, some of Roth's more elaborate custom jobs had caught the public's mood, notably 'The Outlaw', 'Tweedy Pie' and the 'Beatnik Bandit', and other memorable creations, each complete with elaborately painted fibre glass panels and fenders, futuristic dashboards and some even with one-piece moulded Perspex canopies.

Not surprisingly, Revell, depending on the whims and

fancies of a largely youthful market, recognised that this new car craze was an ideal subject for new kits. They quickly realised that Ed Roth might be the ideal ambassador to front a new range.

Consequently, Roth was given a free hand to suggest the best subjects to turn into kits and very soon most of his creations were immortalised in scale plastic. However, Roth didn't stop at customising cars. His fertile mind and peculiar graphic style had invented a range of bizarre cartoon characters to inhabit his far-out world. Soon these too were moulded by Revell to occupy many of his car kits.

Gerry Humbert runs Revell-Monogram's photographic studio. He met Ed Roth on several occasions. He told me the old beatnik was "really out there!"

Once, during a visit to a customising show in Japan, a visitor saw Ed Roth changing out of his grubby, paint-splattered, work overalls as the event was winding down and Roth was preparing to leave for his famous trailer (apparently he rarely stayed in hotels and preferred to live in this temporary home nearby so that he could keep an eye on his precious creations). "Immediately the fan offered Roth $1,000 for his old bib – that was the man's allure!" said Gerry.

Ed Roth will forever be associated with one creation

¹⁄₃₂nd scale DH 'Mosquito IV', 1973.

1973/74 Kit catalogue.

'Huey' and 'Cobra' helicopters from 1967.

above all others – the crazed rodent Ratfink.

With his bulging, blood-shot eyes, manic toothsome gape and pastiche Mickey Mouse ears, Ratfink caught the beatnik mood. He was so successful that Revell quickly produced replicas of Ratfink and his vehicles. Seated in a custom car often adorned with an Iron Cross and or German WWII 'stahlhelm' (two emblems curiously popular with youths at the time) Ratfink became an icon for the alternative youth culture preceding the Punk rock generation.

Incidentally, Ed's 'Big Daddy' soubriquet was apparently invented in the early 1960s by Revell's then head of Public Relations, Henry Blankfurt – a former Hollywood scriptwriter who, like so many others, had fallen foul of the McCarthy blacklist.

Within no time at all Revell were selling millions of Roth's 'funny cars' and monster kits. Some caricatures of Ratfink featured illuminated eyes for added weirdness. The partnership conspired to create healthy profits for Revell and to make Ed Roth a very wealthy man.

I have spoken to many at Revell who had dealings with Roth. All testify to his definite talents and charisma and yes, he did live a very alternative life-style,

entirely living up to his beatnik image.

An uncompromising and very original showman. Roth's ability with pen and brush was held in such esteem that on many occasions when attending trade shows on Revell's behalf, he felt it prudent to accept part-payment in new kits which he would then either sign or decorate to sell to his huge fan base, all eager to own anything inscribed by the hand of the master.

Although he died in 2001, Ed Roth's creations can still be found in model shops and his legacy survives with frequent re-releases of his ideas in model form.

In 1986 Revell merged with that other US Model kit giant, Monogram, and moved from its base in Venice, California to Monogram's home at Morten Grove, a suburb of Chicago.

1976/77 Kit catalogue.

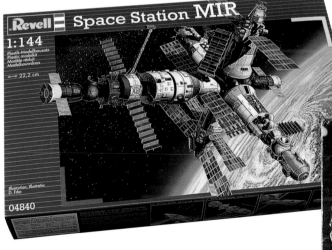

The ill-fated 'MIR'.

¹⁄₁₄₄th scale 007 'Moonraker' Shuttle, 1979.

'Eurofighter' before it became a 'Typhoon'.

Ed Roth's 'Ratfink'.

Revell model kits produced to tie-in with the blockbuster release of 'The Hunt for Red October'.

On a recent visit to Revell-Monogram I was given a tour of the Morten Grove production facility and witnessed kit production and dispatch at the world-famous complex.

Kenneth Funk, Revell-Monogram's Production Manager, has worked at Morten Grove for 25 years. His career began when the facility served only Monogram. In those days he was employed mixing the raw materials – with his hands – which comprised the base ingredients for the particular colour and structural composition of polystyrene chosen for individual kits.

Ken told me that about 2 per cent of the base plastic comprises a colour concentrate and that when he joined Monogram, this colourant was in the form of a messy powder. Apparently, after climbing atop a ladder, this material had to be added in carefully measured handfuls to huge hoppers containing the raw plastic granules that sat above the injection-moulding machines! Today the colourants come in the form of concentrates but, because model enthusiasts prefer to work with white or light grey uncoloured base material, very little is used.

At the time of my visit, in September 2003, to Revell-Monogram at Morten Grove the factory contained 16 state-of-the-art injection-moulding machines, which was far more than I have ever seen assembled on one production floor. Currently the machines operate three shifts and work on a 24-hour basis. Showing me a huge area, which is now used for warehousing and dispatch, Ken told me that this was nothing and that shortly after the merger, the factory contained 44 moulding machines all operating day and night. A sign of the times I suppose. The machines are still in operation around the clock because continuous production is conducive to consistent mould quality. The production facility comprises around 60 staff.

Revell-Monogram's moulding capacity ranges from machines with 75 tons' 'clamping force' to giants which can apply 500 tons' pressure on the enclosed mould tool. Enthusiasts might like to know that the moulded plastic parts, which are removed from one side of the mould as the two halves are separated, are known as a 'shot'. And, contrary to what a lot of 'kit bashers' reckon, 'sprue' is actually the short and thick plug of plastic at the junction of the input feed and the mould itself. This is connected to the 'runners' and their particular 'trees'.

Amazingly, Revell currently uses around 1,000,000 lbs of plastic each year. The Morten Grove facility is home to around 1,000, mostly active, mould tools each of which is carefully stored in an area adjacent to the production floor. Another 2,000 tools are stored ready for use in a nearby storage facility.

Today, a smaller market and fierce competition from overseas means that Revell-

Monogram now outsource much of their production capacity. In the old days Revell would produce as many as 200,000 new kits each month! China is the preferred location for high-volume items. The Chinese are able to provide pre-decorated mouldings and pro-finish pre-painted mouldings at the most competitive price.

The model kit business is an unpredictable animal. Judging forthcoming tastes accurately can be tricky. Like record companies, long-established model manufacturers have the advantage of an enormous back-catalogue of products. Steel mould tools are so substantial that if looked after, they will virtually last forever. Consequently, old models can be re-released with efficiency. The release of James Cameron's movie *Titanic* was a fillip for Revell-Monogram who quickly discovered that they possessed an excellent tool of *Titanic* that was stored amongst the 2,000 kept in reserve. Demand was such that for quite a while the factory was kept in full production churning out this veteran kit around the clock.

Made of machine steel, the original Revell tools are much harder than those made today. However, although they last longer, their toughness makes them very difficult to repair or convert. Many new tools include a beryllium (bronze alloy) component because it is easy to machine and consequently ideal as a base component for the moulding of fine detail and small parts.

Chrome plating is always done remotely from the company's production facility. Revell and Monogram are famous for including such parts in their kits. This specialist process is both messy and toxic. Not surprisingly, many of the firms contracted to do this work also serve the automobile industry – plating the insides of headlamps.

When I visited Morten Grove, two huge halls situated behind the administration, design and marketing offices were divided between moulding, packaging, storage (which includes picking and sorting direct-

ly on to pallets) and dispatch. The palleted cartons are loaded directly into the cavernous containers of articulated lorries that are backed up into loading bays, level with the factory floor, ready for delivery to wholesalers and distributors. The size of this operation is staggering. One can only wonder at what it must have been like at the height of the plastic kit boom in the 1960s and 1970s.

To help me learn more about the US plastic kit industry and Revell-Monogram in particular, I decided that I should make contact with the model giant. Revell's offices in the UK gave me the names of those they thought might be able to help, so I quickly fired off a couple of cries for assistance. Fortunately I didn't have to wait long and very soon arrangements were made for me to visit the home of Revell-Monogram in Chicago.

So, whilst preparing the manuscript for this book I had the great pleasure of being invited to stay at the home of Ed Sexton, Revell-Monogram's Senior Director of Product Development. Ed, his wife Ruan and their

1968 Kit catalogue.

Bell 'X-5', 1960.

Purdey's 'TR7', 1970s.

The Saints' Jaguar 'XJS', 1979.

sibility for assembling the product range each year, compiling the lists of new releases, vintage re-releases and, on occasions, deciding which models will be dropped from the catalogue. He is particularly involved with developing product themes when Revell-Monogram has identified a new category or forecast a fashionable trend.

"A large portion of my job involves licensing," said Ed. "This is intermixed amongst our model range. Basically, I go out and secure fresh licenses, identifying the ones with which we should be most closely involved, and pursuing those we wish to secure."

Ed told me that he is associated with each phase of the marketing cycle. "I am involved in areas such as advertising, creating catalogue entries and have responsibility for the information required on packaging." He is also intimately involved with license contracts. "The way just about all licenses are structured falls within a two to four year range. After the initial two years you may decide to sign a renewal should you wish to continue or, of course, you may decide to drop the new item after two years."

Ed explained the intricacies of the average license agreement: "A percentage royalty, based on the wholesale price is paid on every kit. In addition to this you make an advance payment before you even begin – this might be 24 per cent of what you anticipate the total length of the contract generating in royalties. You also sign a guarantee clause which, regardless of whether you get the product to market or not, commits to an agreed amount of license income." Clearly, Ed's remit is pretty wide ranging.

His earliest memories of plastic kits date from when, at the age of ten or twelve, he visited an older cousin who made WWI aircraft. Ed thinks that they were Aurora kits and particularly remembers 'Fokkers' and 'Sopwith Camels'.

As he grew older, and his cousin moved from the neighbourhood, Ed joined another group of modellers who introduced him to his enduring love –

young son Ted live in a large detached house in the Chicago suburb of Northbrook. This was a short drive from Revell's then HQ at Morten Grove but is even closer to the company's new home in Landwehr St. Ed's home is perfectly positioned from Revell and is a short distance to Chicago's O'Hare airport, which is really useful, as Ed spends time abroad at trade shows and at Revell AG, in Germany.

Although Ed's focus is on the product development side, Revell-Monogram also has a department tasked with evaluating the engineering requirements of each new model and he has to evaluate the budget implications of successive toolings. He also has respon-

Cadillac 'Eldorado', 1956.

'Cherry Pie', 1976.

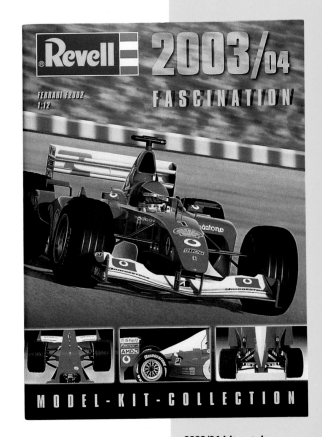

2003/04 kit catalogue, which at the time of writing had sold out.

Austin Powers' 'Corvette Convertible'.

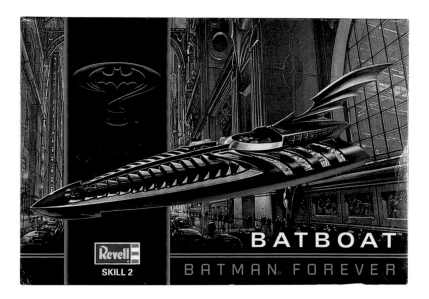

'Bat Boat' from 'Batman Forever'.

The release of the movie 'Rambo' breaths new life into a couple of quite tired Revell kits.

commenced a period of aircraft modelling. This saw him concentrate on US carrier-borne aircraft, characterised by their folding wings and arrester hooks, equipping America's Pacific Fleet following Pearl Harbor. However, as soon as he graduated from college, Ed returned to his first love, automobiles and car models.

Ed told me that during the 1960s, Airfix kits weren't too well known in America. He said that until the early 1970s, the British brand wasn't really much in evidence. However, following a series of visits to the UK, he soon discovered that on this side of the pond 'Airfix' was the generic term for almost any model kit. "They say 'I'm going to build an Airfix. It's like Coke for us!" he laughed. "Although there is a reasonably strong ½nd scale contingent here (Airfix's core scale), America has always been dominated by ¼₈th scale."

Ed first learned of a possible job in the kit industry from Jay Adams, a friend he had first met in a local model shop. Jay worked for Monogram and had what Ed considered 'a really neat job'. After the merger of Revell and Monogram, new owners Odyssey brought the former from its Californian home to Morten Grove, Illinois. Initially, they were careful to maintain each brand's independence and set the two companies apart. Ed told me that the then head of Product Development at Monogram, Bob Johnston, "pretty much went over to the Revell side to manage product development there". Meanwhile Ed's friend Jay had been put in charge of Monogram's product development activities but soon found that the workload there had increased enormously.

Realising this, after about six months, Odyssey told Jay that they were going to recruit someone to help. Needing assistance, and knowing that Ed coveted a job with the famous kit manufacturer, Jay suggested that Ed "fitted the bill exactly" and asked him if he would come in and be interviewed for the new position. Keen modeller Ed jumped at the chance and was immediately hired. He

automobile models. All this occurred in the mid-1960s — the heyday of the North American plastic car model industry.

Whilst at college he dallied with making model aircraft and soon met a fellow student, residing in a nearby dorm, who also made such kits. Unlike Ed, however, this new acquaintance used an airbrush to achieve a superior paint finish. Adopting the instrument himself, Ed soon mastered the intricacies of the airbrush and

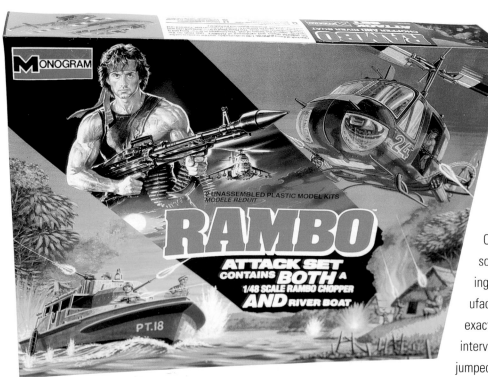

MESSERSCHMITT Bf 109E 1/72 SCALE

MESSERSCHMITT Bf 109E

'ME109E' , 1963.

has worked there since 1989.

I asked Ed about the differences between Revell Inc. in the United Sates and Germany's Revell AG. He told me that although they are both part of the same American holding company, the European and American operations differ quite markedly. In the US, Revell-Monogram sells its products to model distributors and trade arrangements depend on major players buying bulk consignments. In Germany, on the other hand, the relationship is between Revell AG and independent model retailers. Another difference with the 'States is Revell AG's involvement with what is known as 'Pick & Pack' – the breaking of cases of one type of kit and tailoring mixed deliveries to suit a retailer's individual needs. In America this bespoke packing is the responsibility of distributors.

Ed told me that modellers' tastes also differ between Europe and the US. "The subject matter demands are totally different," he said. "Because of this, dating all the way back to the 1960s when Revell Germany was first established, the Continental Europeans have

M.R.C.A. 'Tornado', 1976.

Revell's tribute to the *Kursk*.

Rickenbacker's 'Spad' in
¹⁄₂₅th scale from 1976.

¹⁄₇₂nd scale Sopwith
'Triplane' from 1966.

¹⁄₃₂nd scale 'Typhoon' from
1973 and 'Stuka' in the same
scale from 1972.

enjoyed their own product development, marketing and engineering structures. They function on their own and they decide upon their own range. Consequently, what we both do today is share our individual ranges as required."

Revell Inc. distributes the catalogue printed by Revell AG in Germany and offers its quite different products as a complement to the US range. Ed told me that there was once limited production in England at Potters Bar, but, because of modern communications and sophisticated operating procedures, Revell (GB) is now more involved with sales and administration. "A Revell (GB) salesman simply punches a specific order into a palm pilot and the order is efficiently fulfilled direct from Revell's base in Germany."

F4U-1D CORSAIR

Original Brian Knight box top rough for Revell's ½nd scale F4U-1D Corsair.

Like Airfix, Revell-Monogram regularly re-release vintage kits from yesteryear. Their Selected Subjects Program (SSP) has enabled modellers to rediscover some gems from the 'fifties and 'sixties without paying the high price such 'collectibles' often command. Competitively priced, SSP kits are bought to be constructed. Only the very brave (or fool-hardy) would risk assembling a pristine £300 rarity when there is no guarantee the kit could ever be located again!

Some SSPs are bought by parents who have fond memories of building the particular kit during their child-hood and who are now keen for their children to share their warm memories.

Ed said that, initially, sales of SSP kits were very good. Recently, however, activity has slowed a bit. Ed reckons that this is down to the pent-up demand for the two or three hundred different kits re-released over the years being satisfied. As soon as the 'die-hard' enthusiasts had

bought the SSPs they had long coveted, demand tailed away sharply.

Traditionally, Revell's biggest competitor in its niche market of model cars is, and has always been, America's A.M.T., whose car kits have always given Revell's a run for their money.

Because success in car kits is key to the American market, Revell-Monogram take particular care to ensure that they produce models that will sell. Knowing what the market wants is important and Ed spends a great amount of time listening to the requests of modellers and distributors.

Ed told me that at the time of writing 'Tuners' were very popular – especially Hondas and Subarus into which "kids put ever bigger engines, affix chrome exhausts and add large fibre-glass spoilers on the front ends." Apparently this craze began on the West Coast but has now spread throughout the United States. Ed

Dealer promotion ... "ten-four".

sees it as part of his remit to reflect such interest with each new kit release and thereby satisfy the almost insatiable American demand for automobiles.

Together with Tuners, another popular category for which Revell-Monogram provides an assortment of kits, 'Low-Riders', is proving commercially successful. This fashion started amongst America's Mexican–American community where youngsters would put a set of hydraulics on a car's suspension so that the vehicle body could be raised and lowered – very low.

Low-Rider enthusiasts prefer a certain style of car, particularly old 'sixties Chevys and Bel-airs. The movement is popular enough to support its own magazine and Revell has endeavoured to produce model kits of the most popular Low-Riders seen cruising the streets or at shows and rallies.

Whilst trends such as the fashion for powerful Tuners and Low-Riders might go in and out of vogue, Revell-Monogram feels duty bound to provide replicas of many perennial favourites. Probably the

¹⁄₁₆th scale 1910 'Maxwell', the kit converted from a pull-toy and first available between 1951 and 1955.

Pontiac Club de Mer in ¹⁄₂₅th scale dating from 1957.

most popular of these car models is the 'Mustang'. This car, produced for years in a wide variety of versions, is to Revell-Monogram what the Supermarine 'Spitfire' is to Airfix – a 'banker'. Not content with simply re-releasing popular classics, Revell-Monogram also spends a good deal of its time producing improved versions of kits which have long been popular. A good example of this is Revell's re-tooled '32 Ford 'Hot Rod', an existing kit that sells well to a loyal fan base.

Revell-Monogram does listen to fans and endeavours to catch each successive new wave when it breaks. Indeed they can take pride in appreciating the growing interest in Tuners before their competitors.

They possess an almost unlimited tool bank of vintage kits. The fashion to tune, raise or lower classic American cars means it is relatively easy for the company to select an early tool and make the necessary amendments to the body shell or power plant and very quickly furnish car modellers with the flavour of the month. Only because it has such a rich heritage dating back more than 50 years, possessing dozens of high-quality, tough, machine steel moulds – which would be

virtually impossible to finance from scratch today – can Revell satisfy the changing demands so readily.

"Cars," as Ed told me, "are the core of Revell-Monogram's business." Because they employ real enthusiasts like him, auto fans can rest assured that the company will remain pre-eminent in this field for a long time to come.

When I visited Revell in September 2003, the company was preparing its move to Landwehr Rd. in Northbrook, so things were somewhat in a state of flux. Gerry Humbert, the head of Revell-Monogram's photographic department, has single-handedly managed the switch from film-based technology to digital photography. He prepares all of Revell-Monogram's catalogue and dealer promotion photos in-house using high-resolution studio cameras. Although the digital format has delivered numerous benefits, notably in the area of colour balancing and subject lighting, it has increased Gerry's workload somewhat. The author is partly to

Ed Roth's 1965 'Outlaw' with Robin Hood Fink, in ⅟₂₅th scale.

Ed Roth's 'Surfink' from 1964.

blame. Many of the images of Revell and Monogram kits, especially the earliest ones which I greedily selected from the Morten Grove archive, were photographed by Gerry. Sorry, Gerry, I guess you needed that request like a hole in the head!

Not surprisingly image manipulation has required him to get to grips with a range of computer software, most notably Adobe PhotoShop. Consequently he has also had to familiarise himself with a range of pre-press techniques, previously the province of repro graphics houses, to ensure images are reproduced correctly in print media.

At the time of writing, Revell AG have released their superb ½nd scale U-Boot 'VII C' – I had seen an assembled test shot some months earlier in Chicago. As fans eagerly awaited this enormous masterpiece, Revell AG's website claimed that although this kit had been "frantically awaited", their Junkers 'Ju 290 A-5' long-distance bomber in the same scale and the brand new 'legendary tri-plane' of 'Red Baron' Manfred von Richthofen were to be 'real eye-catchers'.

Like all the great brands, it seems, the secret of Revell's success is never standing still.

¹⁄₁₄₄th scale Laker 'Skytrain' from 1979.

Calypso – complete with miniature helicopter – c'est magnifique.

1932 'V-8 Hot Rod' dating from 1954.

Original Ed Roth
'Outlaw' in ¹⁄₂₅th scale
and dating from 1962.

1957 model
Volkswagen 'Micro
Bus' in ¹⁄₂₅th scale kit
available between
1959 and 1963.

Revell's Douglas 'Thor'
ICBM kit, unusual in
¹⁄₁₁₀th scale, dating from
1959.

ROSEBUD KITMASTER

Kitmaster's ⅟₁₆th scale 'Ariel Arrow' Motorcycle, 1961, soon to join the Airfix range after they acquired Kitmaster at the end of 1962.

Rosebud-Kitmaster is the name of another legendary and short-lived British manufacturer. Their models are high on the 'wants' lists of many collectors.

Founded in 1946 as Nene Plastics Ltd by Londoner Thomas Eric Smith, the son of an east-end toy maker, the new company quickly gained a reputation for the manufacture its high-quality plastic 'Starlight' dolls. Trading as Rosebud, the company gained a reputation for innovation – indeed in 1950 Smith registered two important patents for the manufacture of toy dolls.

In 1958 Rosebud entered the construction kit business. This was partly to utilise excess injection-moulding capacity and partly to jump on the construction kit bandwagon, which was encouraging a host of American manufacturers to flood a ready British market, challenged by only two indigenous manufacturers, Airfix and FROG.

The Rosebud 'Kitmaster' range of construction kits, mostly of locomotives and railway carriages, was of very high quality. The range included examples of some of the earliest railway engines, such as Stephenson's famous 'Rocket'. Miniatures were featured, all to the HO/OO scale established by Frank Hornby, of contemporary engines such as the Battle of Britain class locomotive 'Biggin Hill' and the new 'Deltic' Diesel class of high-speed engines.

Unfortunately for T.E. Smith, the success of the Kitmaster scale model range proved a double-edged sword. It stretched company resources because Kitmaster production drained capacity away from the doll range and also because the expense of running two quite separate types of businesses put an enormous strain on cash flow.

Late in 1962, to preserve the financial integrity of Rosebud, the Kitmaster range was sold to Airfix. Airfix

'Prairie Tank Engine', 1960.

Kitmaster OO-HO gauge 'Evening Star' loco kit.

were enjoying exponential growth and were eager to expand their range by acquisition of existing mould tools.

However, even without kit production, Rosebud's financial difficulties continued, and by 1964 the parent firm was forced into receivership.

The receivers administered the business until 1967 when American giant Mattel bought it. Overnight Rosebud-Mattel Ltd became the world's largest manufacturer of dolls. Incidentally, prior to this, during one of his many travels to North America, T.E. Smith had been offered and had *declined* the opportunity to manufacture G.I. Joe under license in the UK. General Mill's British subsidiary Palitoy ultimately became the lucky hosts of the British version ... Action Man.

The Rosebud brand name finally disappeared in 1971.

Because the Kitmaster range of model kits existed for only five years, surviving

models are scarce and highly sought after by collectors. Most, but not all, of Kitmaster's products were issued by Airfix and many collectors look for examples of identical models under each brand name. Despite being more than 40 years old, surviving examples of Kitmaster trains (they also originated Airfix's famous 'Ariel Arrow' motorcycle – a curious one-off) are of surprisingly high quality and are capable of giving some modern kits a real run for their money.

Kitmaster rebuilt 'Royal Scot'.

Kitmaster '2nd Class carriage'.

Kitmaster '1st Class Restaurant car'.

SKYBIRDS

Arguably the British firm of 'Skybirds', founded by one James Hay Stevens, manufactured the earliest construction kits of the format we take for granted today.

In the 1930s and 40s, Stevens was a celebrity author and illustrator amongst aviation enthusiasts. His drawings for George Newnes' magazine *Air Stories* had brought him to prominence amongst the 'air minded' youngsters who followed every development in Britain's rapidly expanding aircraft industry which was frantically re-arming as conflict with Hitler's Germany loomed.

Stevens is not only rightly famous as an illustrator and writer, amongst plastic modellers he is recognised as the founder

Press ad for Skybirds 'World-Famous Aeronautical Models' dating from 1938.

of ½nd scale. In this scale a miniature 1″ represents 6′ of the full-size object. Stevens' system was very quickly adopted by British aircraft modellers. At home, and internationally, it was also chosen as the scale for 'recognition models' used by civil defence forces and anti-aircraft gunners to learn the difference between the silhouettes of friend or foe.

Ironically, Stevens' art was to be a major influence on the young Roy Cross who was later to be famous as, perhaps, Airfix's premier box top artist. Fittingly, like Roy Cross, Stevens has also earned a place in the modellers' hall of fame.

Initially releasing a tiny replica of the RAF's 'Cierva Autogyro' – a kind of helicopter/aircraft hybrid – by 1935 the Skybirds range amounted to some 20 models. Amongst them was a DH 'Puss Moth', famous for its long-distance flights when piloted by Amy Johnson.

Skybirds' range also included the Hawker 'Hart' which, with the 'Hind' and 'Gladiator', comprised the trio of old-fashioned RAF biplanes expected to confront the might of the Luftwaffe immediately before the advent of the 'Spitfire' and 'Hurricane'.

In 'Series No 7' the Skybirds Fokker 'DVII' was typical of their products. It comprised a finely crafted, contoured fuselage and aerofoil-profiled wings with brass wheels and tailskid, acetate tail and elevator unit, and a sachet of glue in powder form – 'mix 1 part glue and 2 parts water and boil for 10 minutes'. Emery paper 'for wood work' was also included.

The exigencies of wartime production and his involvement in the war effort put paid to Stevens' model-manufacturing business. Anyway, by the late 1930s the cheaper and more accurate 'Penguin' kits from IMA were already challenging Skybirds' position.

Skybirds' delightful Fokker DVII kit from the mid-1930s. James Hay Stevens' 'Givjoy' brand is responsible for the established scale of ½nd and also for producing a range of multi-media (mixed materials not 'interactive'!) which top most collectors' 'wants' lists. They can be found but, not surprisingly, they are very, very expensive.

TAMIYA

Mr Shunsaku Tamiya.

Photo of the Tamiya Shoji & Co premises in September 1951. Standing in front of the recently rebuilt factory is Chairman Yoshio Tamiya, Shunsaku's father.

Before the introduction of plastic injection-moulding technology to Japan after the Second World War, Japanese craft toys and models had always been made from indigenous timbers like Japanese Cypress, Magnolia and Katsura.

Shizuoka-City, a suburb of Tokyo, had long been the centre for the manufacture of these artifacts. Along with numerous timber yards and finishing mills the area boasted the highest concentration of craftsmen skilled in the precision assembly of fine wooden products. Not surprisingly these skilled artisans were ideally suited to the switch in manufacturing techniques that was introduced during the mid-1950s to replace the smashed machinery of a defeated Japan. Consequently, Shizuoka-City became the location for the introduction of the latest injection-moulding technology, which transformed local industrial capacity as factories abandoned wood and began producing products made from plastic. Today, almost all of Japan's plastic construction kit manufac-

turers among them Aoshima, Hasegawa, Fujimi and Imai, are based in the area.

However, of them all, Tamiya is pre-eminent and today enjoys an unrivalled reputation as the finest firm of its kind anywhere in the world.

Like many of its competitors, Tamiya started life in the lumber business. In 1946 Mr Yoshio Tamiya founded a wood yard and saw mill in Shizuoka-City. Within a year his business had begun to exploit the market for high-quality wooden model kits. These construction kits were so successful that in 1953 the decision was made to close the timber yard and concentrate entirely on wooden kits.

Elsewhere though the trend was towards construction kits moulded from plastic. These proved enormously popular in Europe and especially the US. Here manufacturers like Revell and Monogram had discovered that consumers preferred to avoid a lot of the preparatory labour demanded by traditional wooden kits and eagerly snapped up the new plastic replicas which almost immediately resembled their intended subjects.

Yoshio Tamiya's son, Shunsaku, encountered his first plastic construction kit in 1958. It was a Revell import — a tank — and it was a revelation. Previously, Shunsaku, a keen scale modeller, had been forced to fashion tank wheels from miniature pulleys and to form gun barrels from aluminium tubing. In the ⅟₈₀th scale kit box before him, Shunsaku discovered finely moulded plastic pieces — wheels, gun barrel, turret and tracks of a far higher quality than any amount of woodcarving could hope to mimic. Although common today, in 1950s Japan polystyrene was a scarce and expensive commodity. Strictly controlled American imports were also an expensive luxury.

In his book *Master Modeller* Shunsaku Tamiya recalls the effort and financial outlay needed to acquire examples of foreign kits before Japan's prodigious plastics manufacturing revolution in the early sixties.

In 1959, convinced that the future of model manufacture lay in the production of plastic kits and with orders for their traditional wooden models falling away alarmingly, Shunsaku persuaded his father to take the bold step of switching to polystyrene injection-moulding.

A replica of the famous Japanese battleship *Musashi* was the subject chosen for the first Tamiya injection-moulded kit. Previously, when wooden models were all the rage in Japan, Tamiya was affectionately known as 'the warship company', so the choice of subject seemed appropriate.

Pre-production planning of a plastic kit required far more effort than was involved with simpler wooden

¹⁄₃₅th scale German Infantry from Tamiya's famous 'Military Miniatures' range.

Original Tamiya packaging for the cruiser *Atago*.

¹⁄₈₀₀th scale Yamato box art.

models. Fortunately, to help prepare the component drawings required to facilitate mould production, Tamiya secured the efforts of Hatsuji Shinomiya, a local warship enthusiast.

The painful learning curve required by the transition from wood to plastic meant adopting new techniques and out-sourcing a number of key processes that were then alien to Tamiya's traditional work force. The most conspicuously demanding service in terms of both money and effort was contracting a suitable moulding house. In the late 1950s, Japanese injection moulders had a surfeit of work and were in constant demand.

After imploring a suitable moulding house to accept the commission for the *Musashi* mould tool and agreeing to punitive payment terms and an unreasonable delivery schedule, Tamiya could do nothing but hope for the best. Anyway, in Japan at that time, moulding houses preferred simpler industrial contracts – Tamiya's request for so many finely detailed and fiddly pieces was hardly alluring. Tamiya even had to pay over the odds for imported raw plastic, Japanese material at the time being generally of poor quality.

In 1960 Tamiya's first plastic construction kit was at last ready. It was

in a box emblazoned with the company's new identity, designed by Shunsaku's art-student brother Masao.

Unfortunately rival Nichimo had made similar plans and had managed to get their model, also of the battleship *Musashi*, into the shops ahead of Tamiya's. It was also on sale for a lot less than Tamiya had planned to ask for their kit. Furthermore the rival's kit came with a pre-coloured hull that was red below the waterline. Although of a smaller scale, Nichimo's model outsold Tamiya's.

Forced to recycle their expensive mould and re-issue it as *Yamato*, the sister ship of *Musashi*, Tamiya braced themselves. This model fared little better and Tamiya sank further and further into debt.

After temporarily revisiting the wooden model business with almost inevitable futility, Tamiya considered releasing warships moulded from buoyant Styrofoam. This was viewed as too flimsy by Japanese enthusiasts and its lack of substance proved a non-starter.

Just as things looked desperate, Tamiya was saved by a happy accident. Shunsaku Tamiya was offered some second-hand moulds for a range of cheap toy cars and trucks – novelties of the kind given away as confectionery premiums in Japan.

Having agreed the purchase of the tools, Shunsaku called his new models 'Baby Racers' and packaged them in boxes decorated with illustrations he had scoured from coloured advertisements and

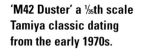

'M42 Duster' a ¹⁄₃₅th scale Tamiya classic dating from the early 1970s.

articles in American glossy magazines.

To everyone at Tamiya's surprise, the Baby Racers sold like hot cakes. These low cost mini-kits, which actually rolled along a flat or sloped surface, caught the attention of Japanese youth. Shunsaku decided it was time to return to the manufacture of plastic construction kits proper.

Boldly, this time Tamiya decided to move away from warships, the very subject that had made the company's name in its heyday. Shunsaku opted to produce a model tank.

The German WWII 'Panther' was the chosen subject, its angular lines and clean surfaces ideally lending themselves to injection moulding and featuring none of the myriad complexities of a warship. Shunsaku decided to add an electric motor, something rival American kits lacked at the time. However, his major coup was in securing the talents of the famous Japanese illustrator Shigeru Komatsuzaki to prepare the box top illustration.

Shunsaku Tamiya was determined that his new 'Panther' kit would restore the company's fortunes. No stone was left unturned to ensure perfection. At the time, Japanese instruction leaflets left a lot to be desired, being imprecise in almost every detail. With

Original packaging for the 'Panther Tank' kit which was available from New Year 1962. The stirring artwork is by the hand of Shigeru Komatsuzaki.

¹⁄₃₅th scale British WWII 'Cromwell MkIV'.

Exquisite ¹⁄₃₅th scale replica of the Wehrmacht's novel 'Schwimmwagen' amphibious vehicle. Released in the late nineteen-nineties this model was a great improvement on Tamiya's earlier kit from the 'seventies. It was soon supplemented by a great accessory set of figures based on the famous photo alleged to depict Joachim Peiper and members of his eponymous 'Kampfgruppe' in the Ardennes during the 'Battle of the Bulge' in 1944.

Inaugural edition of *Tamiya Model Magazine*.

100th edition of *Tamiya Model Magazine*.

the bit between his teeth, Shunsaku decided to prepare the new instructions in the American 'exploded view' style and draw them himself.

The model 'Panther' was finally ready for sale by New Year 1962. A great deal rested on its success.

Tamiya needn't have worried. It sold by the thousand and repeat orders flooded in. These were often difficult to fulfil on time – even with Shunsaku and his employees driving the delivery truck! An added bonus for purchasers was that the gearbox driven by the miniature electric motor had a higher gear ratio than rival kits and the Tamiya tank regularly won any neighbourhood challenges.

With the release of their 'Panther' kit, Tamiya established a reputation for top quality, exemplified by Komatsuzaki's superior box art. They also stole a march on competitors because of the quality of their motorisation. Although not the province of this book, remote and radio control-powered models are still a huge percentage of Tamiya's income. Enthusiasts will be familiar with the eternal success of Tamiya's miniature four-wheel drive models (the 'Mini 4WD Series') and their long involvement in larger ⅛th scale Radio Control (RC) vehicles. The combination of this long heritage in fine scale modelling and precision electronics and miniature motorisation has recently reached its peak with the release of Tamiya's superb 1⁄16th scale tanks. These motorised 'Tigers' and 'Shermans' even come complete with servo-controlled turrets, guns which recoil upon firing and sound boxes which mimic the distinctive steel roar and rattle of full-sized armoured leviathans.

The original 'Panther' kit also firmly established 1⁄35th as the standard scale for the majority of Tamiya's military vehicles and accessories. In fact the choice of this scale was almost accidental. It was adopted because it enabled the chosen electric motor to sit most comfortably within the 'Panther's' hull!

Tanks appeared to point the way forward. Very quickly the company produced more and more and is now probably most associated with this type of kit. Their classic 'World Tank' series of motorised WWII AFVs, from the 1960s and early-1970s, have now become collectors' items.

As they expanded Tamiya could no longer rely entirely on the output of free-lance artists like Komatsuzaki, so they decided to establish their own in-house training school and graphics facility. Together with Komatsuzaki, famous Tamiya artists such as Masami Onshi and Yoshiyuki Takani have conspired to create Tamiya's uniquely memorable style.

In 1963 Tamiya's first plastic aircraft kit, a ⅟₅₀th replica of Japan's famous 'Zero' fighter, was released. Apparently, for Japanese enthusiasts the design of its only real competitor, a 'quarter-scale' (⅟₄₈th) model by Chicago's Monogram, did not entirely capture the subtle lines of Mitsubishi's masterpiece.

Tamiya's Model 52 'Zero' Fighter, with box art again produced by the legendary Komatsuzaki, arrived in the shops in June 1963. It was received to wide acclaim and finally proved that homegrown Japanese product could compete head on with well-established manufacturers from overseas.

Tamiya's 'Zero' was the first scale replica to capture

Tamiya catalogue 1984 edition.

faithfully the aircraft's shape and established firmly a tradition of accuracy and precision which is today second to none. Incidentally, upholding this tradition, enthusiasts will know that recently Tamiya have released another 'Zero' fighter. This one, a type 'A6M5' in large ⅟₃₂nd scale is surely the definitive injection-moulded kit of this machine.

Ships, tanks and aircraft – the definitive Tamiya combination. The great company was on course.

By the mid-1960s Tamiya began to investigate the possibility of bringing mould making – the one weak link in their

⅟₂₀th scale 'Tyrrell P34' six-wheeled F1 racecar.

supply chain – in-house. Although contracting out for such specialist services was the norm, each time a new tool was required Tamiya were forced to endure a price rise and almost unbearable delivery terms.

Gradually the company established a cadre of young trainees who were each given plenty of time to learn the intricacies of this highly skilled business by enrolling on college courses or being apprenticed to master technicians at bespoke moulding houses. Shunsaku Tamiya convinced his somewhat sceptical father that the company should at least put its toes in the water of this complex process by investing in sufficient hardware to enable the company to at least repair and renovate its existing moulds.

Almost by a process of osmosis Tamiya developed the in-house skills and technological base to enable the establishment of its own Moulding Division. Quickly this

department established standards to which other manufacturers could only aspire.

In 1968 Tamiya produced their first set of ⅟₃₅th scale soldiers, a squad of German infantry, the ideal accompaniment for the growing range of predominantly German vehicles. Although not up to the standards of more modern releases, this set, and the box of US Troops that soon followed, sold tremendously well. Actually Tamiya subsequently perfected the anatomical poses of their figures by collaborating with the celebrated Japanese animator, Yasuo Otsuka, who had precisely studied the human form and especially how it moves as part of his particular art.

Tamiya kits became a huge success and before the decade was over the company had the honour of being the first Japanese model kit manufacturer to exhibit at the prestigious Nuremberg Toy Fair.

Tamiya diorama showing Famo, Kubelwagen and Wehrmacht soldiers.

The success of Tamiya's military miniatures generated requests for the firm to produce a range of smaller vehicles and scale figures to accompany them. I well remember searching for the latest Tamiya kit at BMW Models, the famous Wimbledon model shop, or at Jones Bros of Turnham Green in Chiswick. These were two of the handful of 'real' model shops where, in the early days, one could be sure to find Tamiya's fine models. The advent of 'Beatties' made things even simpler.

Readers might recall that for most of this period Tamiya kits were imported and distributed by Richard Kohnstam (RIKO) whose David Binger enjoyed a close working relationship with Shunsaku Tamiya from 1966 until the latter retired

⅛th scale metal German 'Wehrmacht Squad Leader'.

Diorama featuring ⅓₅th scale 'M26 Pershings'.

It's a call for you.

30 years later. Incidentally, Richard Kohnstam could trace his family's origins in the toy business back to 1890. By the mid-fifties, amongst numerous other toy distribution agreements, Kohnstam was closely involved with Matchbox die-casts (see above), incorporating his own 'Moko' trade mark on Lesney packaging and at one point even owning the trademark registration of the 'Matchbox' brand!

Answering market demand in 1970 Tamiya produced a tiny ⅟₃₅th scale replica of Germany's wartime 'Schwimmwagen' amphibious patrol car. Today numerous ⅟₃₅th scale support vehicles, armoured and soft skinned, from every major international conflict since 1939 and dozens of figure and diorama accessories comprise Tamiya's huge military miniature range.

Since the early days, Tamiya has provided a host of

The groundbreaking ⅟₁₆th scale radio-controlled 'Tiger 1'.

support services to modellers. The first edition of *Tamiya News,* the company's magazine for modellers, was a modest 16-page affair. Printed in Japanese, it was intended to provide modellers with articles, hints and tips about particular kits, supplementary to the information printed on the instruction leaflet.

Shunsaku Tamiya hoped to mirror the success of Britain's *Airfix Magazine,* which he considered an extremely valuable reference work and which particularly impressed him because of its impartiality and readiness to consider the merits of a rival manufacturer's products. Despite its small size Shunsaku considered *Airfix Magazine* an excellent publication and was confident that Tamiya should sponsor a publication of equally high standard.

Although, Shunsaku probably didn't know it at the

time, the reason that *Airfix Magazine* pursued such an egalitarian course had little to do with benevolence. Ralph Ehrmann, Airfix Chairman during the company's 'glory years', told me recently that by the late sixties his financial advisers had told him that with 60 per cent of the home market and growing international sales, Airfix was in danger of monopolising the kit industry to an unhealthy extent which might lead to the demise of competitors and, ultimately, a decline of interest in the hobby as whole. For plastic modelling to keep growing there had to be a commercially viable industry in which others would trade.

Consequently, *Airfix Magazine* was encouraged to review the products of rival firms. I well remember the glowing reviews in the magazine for many of Tamiya's products (their celebration of the superb ⅟₂₅th scale

Centurion tank comes to mind) that began to appear with increasing regularity in the early 1970s.

Incidentally, enthusiasts might also be interested to learn that Ralph Ehrmann told me that Airfix's decision to begin their ⅟₃₂nd scale range of AFV models, beginning with the 'Crusader' tank, was a direct result of the impact of Tamiya's superbly detailed military models. However, after they commenced their new range, the sales volumes for the Airfix models were so low that they simply couldn't understand how Tamiya could make the formula work!

Airfix Magazine has long gone but the publication of *Tamiya Model Magazine*, which now appears in several international editions, has more than filled the void.

The inaugural edition of *Tamiya Model Magazine* was published in the UK early in 1985. On the cover it sported

German 18t 'Famo' half-track released in 1999.

a fine model of Tamiya's, then, new *USS Enterprise* aircraft carrier. This kit, in Tamiya's larger ⅟₃₅₀th scale (their 'waterline' vessels are in smaller ⅟₇₀₀th) was a revelation of super detail and moulding finesse. At over a metre in length the finished kit probably also required modellers who had chosen to build it to move house in order to find room to display it! At the time of writing (August 2003) *Tamiya Model Magazine* had just celebrated its 100th edition in the UK and has consistently upheld the tradition of excellence for which Tamiya is widely recognised.

Through the good offices of Mr Yasushi Sano I had the great pleasure of meeting Tamiya's President and Chairman, Mr Shunsaku Tamiya at Chicago's 2003 Model & Hobby Expo. This show takes place early in September. Mr Tamiya told me that when he and his colleagues left Chicago on September 11th, 2001, they were surprised when their Boeing '747' suddenly turned about and headed back towards O'Hare airport. Little did they know then that they were airborne at precisely the same moment that

the terrorist atrocity was occurring in New York.

After watching an exciting demonstration involving a radio-controlled duel between Tamiya's ⅟₁₆th scale 'Sherman' and 'Tiger' tanks – complete with sound effects – I was ushered into a meeting area on Tamiya's Expo stand. Plastic kit enthusiasts can take comfort in the fact that the gentleman is as enthusiastic about kits today as he ever was. Although reluctant to pick any favourites, when pressed Mr Tamiya chose one or two of his kits that he especially likes. Mr Tamiya is especially fond of his company's ⅟₃₅₀th scale *Prince of Wales* British battleship kit. Incidentally he told me that to ensure accuracy with their similarly scaled kit of the German pocket-battleship *Bismarck*, Tamiya had to refer to documents captured by the Soviets. Apparently the advancing Red armies overran much of the Third Reich's maritime administration and secured most of the Kriegsmarine's plans and archives. It was only glasnost and the thaw in east–west relations, which enabled Tamiya's designers to study the

Superlative ¼₈th scale 'Fairey Swordfish' torpedo bomber from 1999.

original shipwright drawings – such is Tamiya's quest for accuracy.

Amongst other personal favourites, which include many armoured fighting vehicles – notably Tamiya's larger scale 'Tiger' tanks and especially the famous 'King Tiger' – Shunsaku Tamiya naturally has a soft spot for one kit in particular. Fittingly perhaps this is a replica of a Japanese classic, Tamiya's superb ⅓₂nd scale 'A6M5 Zero' Fighter that comes with full internal detail

and many multi-media parts to help achieve the definitive model of such a great fighter plane. Fans will know that Tamiya sponsor a tank hall at England's famous museum at Bovington.

I have followed the, at times, stunning progress of Tamiya since I bought my first Tamiya kits in the early 1970s. I remember that they were boxes of 'Military Miniatures' Afrika Korps, US Infantry and three British Tommies laying the venerable 6-pounder anti-tank gun.

The memorable ⅛th scale 'Lancaster BI/BIII' from 1975.

Doing justice to Mitsubishi's classic at last – ⅓₂nd scale 'Zero A6M4'.

Tamiya's awesome ⅟₃₅₀th scale carrier *USS Enterprise*.

Famous artist Shigeru Komatsuzaki during the early years.

A while later I bought Tamiya's lovely ⅟₃₅th scale Kettenkraftrad – the ingenious motorcycle/half track combination Wehrmacht soldiers used to good effect on the snow-covered steppes of Russia. I recalled that when originally issued it came with an engine cast in white metal. "Indeed you are correct," said my mentor at Tamiya, the ever-helpful Yasushi Sano. "At the time of first release (August 1973), the model had a metal engine, but later switched to a plastic engine. I am not quite sure what was the real reason for the switch, but as an average modeller, I guess that back then many of us lacked the proper glue (instant cement, epoxy, etc.) to bond these (additional) parts together." Mr Sano told me that these metal castings were made in Hong Kong, and not in Japan.

Tamiya's memorable ⅟₂₅th German Metal Figures were

An assortment of Tamiya's famous ¹⁄₇₀₀th scale 'Waterline' warships.

Computer-aided design
(CAD) in Tamiya's
design division.

Tamiya injection-
moulding machine in
operation.

NC milling machine in
Tamiya's tooling
division.

Overview of tooling
division.

also produced by their Hong Kong manufacturer. These figures were excellent and belied some of the criticism at the time about the lack of anatomical finesse in many of Tamiya's accessory figures.

"I think there are several reasons for discontinuing this series," said Yasushi Sano. "Firstly a similar reason to the above item, which is the lack of good cement. The lack of good primer for metal parts could also be a reason. Secondly, many modellers back then were a little discouraged to find that it was just a blown-up version from a ⅓₅th scale figure. Thirdly, building just the figures was not that popular back then with our Japanese audiences. They could be used for accompanying our ¹⁄₂₅th

tanks, but that is about it."

Yasushi Sano pointed out that at the time Tamiya, and Japanese modellers in general, were into motorising their kits rather than incorporating them into diorama settings – accessories like figures were somewhat superfluous. "You may remember that we re-released all the four figures plus six more in a plastic version in the early eighties," he added. These plastic miniatures were far cheaper than their metal predecessors and sold rather better which "indicated the difficulty of selling metal figures back then," he told me. The earlier cost hike for metal models made "a big price difference for kids," he said.

However, collectors haven't been forgotten. In November 2003 Yasushi Sano told me that because they retain the original tooling, Tamiya intend re-issuing those four metal figures again "this winter" in the original boxes.

By a combination of long-term planning, investment in the latest technology, innovative employee training schemes and, of course, legendary attention to detail and scale accuracy, Shunsaku Tamiya has built a company that has become the watchword for excellence in the kit industry. I'm sure his father would be very proud.

⅓₅th German 'Army Tank' crew set dating from 1968.

3. Genres

Some plastic modellers make miniature replicas of anything that takes their fancy, choosing subjects which include aircraft, military vehicles, figures, ships, cars, railways or space and fantasy vehicles.

However most enthusiasts specialise in one particular field. To be any good takes an awful lot of practice and the techniques required to make the best of a particular model can vary radically from genre to genre. For example, military modellers expend enormous energy 'weathering' tanks and lorries; adding rust streaks, paint chips or exhaust stains and often dusting the lower bodies of vehicles with powders to simulate the wear and tear of war machines in the action.

Car modellers, on the other hand, work hard to achieve the smoothest paint finishes, spraying and rubbing down only to re-spray and repeat the process in an effort to capture that elusive high gloss finish on a showroom vehicle.

Aircraft modellers will airbrush complicated matt camouflage schemes only to cover them with gloss varnish to ensure the adhesion of water-slide decals and then finally apply a matt coat.

For a long time in the figure modelling area there has been a healthy debate about the merits of enamel and oil-based paints. And now, acrylics have migrated from aircraft modellers and they have entered the fray. Regardless, most figure modellers generally agree that artist's oil paint is best for skin tones, despite the much longer drying times.

Different kinds of models require a great deal of very particular technical application. Little wonder then, that generally, modellers stick to type.

I thought that one of the best people to ask about the current state of the hobby would be the affable Paul Regan, currently President of the International Plastic Modellers Society (IPMS) UK. The IPMS is a truly global phenomenon, a vibrant forum where like-minded plastic modellers can meet to compete and discuss the latest developments in the hobby. They might also learn one or two trade secrets from fellow members, many of whom are masters of their art.

Lindberg ½th scale 'Search & Rescue CB Patrol Vehicle'.

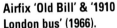

Airfix 'Old Bill' & '1910 London bus' (1966).

"I am a bit of a rarity in the modelling world as I started when I was six (Airfix series one 'Typhoon', bought at Woolworth's in Sandbach on a rainy Thursday – I still have the model!), and have never stopped, managing to continue for the last 34 years without any breaks," Paul told me. "I joined IPMS in 1983, joined the National Committee in 1993 and was elected as President at the AGM in April 2002.

"I do not consider myself a collector as I fully intend to build the kits that I buy. However, when I moved into my current house, I took the opportunity to count the boxes as they were located into the loft, and the figure (adjusted for those bought since) means that I have approx 4,500 'kits' of one form or another in the loft as of December 2003.

"I have never really specialised in a single area of modelling, and thus although aircraft undoubtedly predominate, there are significant quantities of military vehicles, cars, some ships, and a considerable quantity of Science Fiction and Fantasy amongst them. Similarly, although most are straight injection-moulded plastic, there are (very) many vac forms, resin and metal items amongst the piles."

Hubley Mercedes '300 SL' (1960s).

MPC Camaro 'Z28'.

Airfix motor vehicle assortment.

Snap Fit 'Flintmobile' from the 'Flintstone's' movie (1994).

1/25th Revell Charlie's Angels 'Mobile Unit Van' (1977).

Scale Models **magazine's "Power Crisis' edition (March 1974). How many readers remember the coal shortages, power cuts and the three-day week?**

Paul works as a Commercial Manager for a packaging organisation, a vocation that he says has enabled him both to indulge his hobby and let him achieve a 'lifelong ambition' of securing a Private Pilot's Licence.

"The International Plastic Modellers Society was formed in late 1963 in the United Kingdom, and the UK organisation is still seen both as the founding father of the organisation worldwide and the body to which the overseas Branches look for leadership," he told me. "Despite the vagaries of the hobby, it is quite surprising that the membership of the Society has remained fairly constant for many years now, at between 1,500 and 2,000 here in the UK.

"We have a Branch network covering the UK consisting of some 55 Branches with 50 Special Interest Groups (SIGs – groupings of modellers who have an interest in certain types of modelling – civil airliners, warships, etc). There are around 45 International Groups around the world, which in turn have their own Branches and SIGs. It is definitely true that IPMS is the home of the true model enthusiast."

"The kit industry in the 21st Century has changed considerably from what was probably its heyday in the 1960s and 1970s, when it briefly had something of a mass-market appeal. In those days (when, I must add, I was a child so some memories are maybe a little 'rose-tinted'), it was possible to buy kits pretty well anywhere – the local paper shop, Post Office, hardware shop (before the modern DIY depots of course!) and sports shops all had limited displays of kits, and there was of course Woolworth's which seemed to have a new Airfix item each week.

"Even my relatively small town had 'The Model and Toy Shop' (note the sequence in the title), which held what would be regarded as a pretty good stock even with today's fragmented market, with kits from all the then important manufacturers – Airfix, FROG, Tamiya, Matchbox, Hasegawa and Monogram (strangely, I don't recall Revell much in those days), plus a complete range of paints, books, tools, scenic materials and some transfers.

"Nowadays, I live in the somewhat larger city of Leeds, within which kits can be obtained from perhaps a dozen outlets in total, with only a small handful who stock more than 'starter sets' and the basic ranges. Most will sell you some glue, and some may even have some paints … but certainly not very many. Sadly, as with most modern retailing, even in so-called toy shops, kits are sold as 'S.K.U.' (Stock Keeping Units for those not familiar with retail speak) by staff who know nothing of their product and, being honest, have no interest in them – indeed, this may be true of some of the members of the kit industry itself.

"This move has mirrored changes within the manufacturers of kits themselves, with the collapse of many of the original founding fathers of the hobby and with some of the names simply dropping out of sight altogether. Others have disappeared and reappeared, and a small number have apparently prospered. At the same time a huge explosion of smaller manufacturers, in particular from the ex-Eastern Bloc countries, has occurred, although the availability and longevity of some of these is questionable.

"However, what has happened has been a radical and rapid growth in the so-called 'cottage industry', which originally appeared back in the 1980s, initially concentrating on providing the modeller with options for markings and some small detail parts. Gradually, these small producers have increased their products and have also moved into producing their own complete kits, many of them being of subjects which the 'mainstream' producers would never contemplate, and produced to standards which could never be commercially viable."

I asked Paul to tell me how all of these moves have been echoed by the hobby and the modellers who

follow it. "I suspect that the reduced sales of kits are reflected by the fact that even the enthusiasts are producing fewer finished models themselves nowadays," he said. "For instance, where modellers used to produce models almost on a production-line basis – more or less straight out of the box – nowadays, they seem to be spending increasing amounts of time and money on conversion parts, decals, etc., to produce a masterpiece. In many cases, they do not even use kits as the starting point, with competitions usually being dominated by scratch-built masterpieces. The industry reflects this in the growth of the cottage industry, and in the rise of the super kit, with mainstream manufacturers putting etched metal, resin and metal parts into their kits in the pursuit of ever more highly detailed results – at a price.

"Fortunately for the industry most modellers are very unrealistic as to their actual building capabilities, which has resulted in virtually all of them moving into the kit collector category over the years. This seems to sneak up on people, usually beginning with just buying new products as they are released. The intent is always to

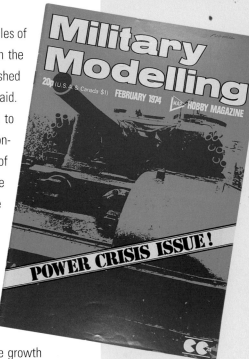

Military Modelling magazine's crisis issue (February 1974).

Selection of Merit railway accessories.

Matchbox challenge Airfix's market in soft plastic soldiers.

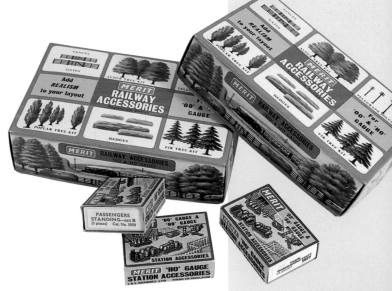

build the models purchased, then it becomes a case of buying them in case they disappear again quickly – perhaps enhanced by the way that quite a few products are limited editions, specifically to appeal to this instinct."

Paul told me that different modellers buy kits for very personal reasons. Some, because they are committed to completing a variety of aircraft or vehicles within a particular series or depicting a period within a famous military campaign. Others, rather aimlessly, just because the new model is the 'latest'.

Paul, however, is pretty focused. "I will continue to buy every aeroplane kit which Airfix release regardless of subject ... but I still intend to get around to building them all, eventually."

As one might expect, many prominent plastic modellers are proficient in more than one category, happily building a military vehicle one week and following this with an aircraft model the next. However, it is generally the case that individual modellers choose a par-

ticular theme and stick with it. One of the by-products of making construction kits is discovering more about the subject you have chosen to model. Learning more about specific operational details encourages a more accurate build. It often surprises non-modellers to discover that far from sitting alone for hours on end, achieving little more than a completed model and a pallid complexion, many enthusiasts involve themselves in a wide range of research activities, some of which include visits to far-flung battlefields, museums or airfields.

Whilst briefly studying the broadly separate themes modellers choose to pursue, I've linked the following well-known modellers with the subject area they are most closely associated with.

I've decided to begin with military modelling, my preferred theme (son of a soldier and all that).

When, in 1970 I began to take scale modelling more seriously, the same names featured time and again in Britain's three main plastic modelling titles, *Airfix*

Nichimo 'Spitfire' – *the* Royal Air Force Fighter!

Magazine, *Military Modelling* and *Scale Models*.

In those days the names of John Sandars, Chris Ellis, Ken Jones and Roy Dilley were frequently associated with articles about armoured fighting vehicles or utility 'soft skin' lorries and 'Jeeps'. These gentlemen showed readers how to convert commercially available models of military vehicles, almost always based on the ubiquitous and cheap Airfix HO/OO range, or for the more adventurous amongst us, how to 'scratch build' from scale plans.

Scratch building consumed sheets of thin plastic card, which could be purchased in a variety of thicknesses and were measured in thousandths of an inch. With the advent of the early liquid cements such as 'Mek Pak', modellers were at last able to assemble models constructed of the most delicate polystyrene components. Their patience was rewarded with true scale appearance, something that even the best efforts of kit designers and toolmakers could rarely achieve with injection moulding.

Following the revolution in precision and scale heralded by the arrival of Tamiya's larger ⅓₅th models in the early 1970s, other military modellers came to prominence. Foremost amongst them were 'Mac' Kennaugh, Bill Evans and, of course, Francois Verlinden. Although modellers like Roy Dilley had long espoused the advantages of displaying figures or vehicles in a suitable diorama setting – showing tyros how to make terrain from 'Plaster of Paris' and fashion flock grass, so often the province of railway modellers, to create miniature landscapes – the honour of elevating the craft to an art really goes to Mr Verlinden.

In the mid-seventies, from his Belgian home, models by Verlinden regularly graced the pages of the British modelling press. He won award after award for his imaginative set pieces, each of which featured his unique approach to weathering and animation. Francois owned a successful hobby shop in Belgium, from where his 'VP' range of plaster accessories were received to wide acclaim, and had already started publishing a series of books illustrating his very

accomplished techniques. In the early 1980s, award-winning American modeller Bob Letterman and Dutch investor Jos Stok joined forces with Verlinden. In 1985 the trio combined their talents and founded the VLS Corporation in Missouri, USA. It has developed into one of the biggest model and hobby operations worldwide, nurturing many successful offshoots and a thriving e-commerce business, modelmecca.com.

Francois Verlinden was one of the first proponents of

One of the popular range of 'Dog Fight Doubles'.

Starting with the release of their ½th scale Coldstream Guardsman figure in 1959 right up to their superb rendition of a Napoleonic Imperial Guard in 1976, Airfix have produced an enviable back catalogue of military figures in this large scale. The figure of the Emperor himself, seen here assembled, courtesy of John Wells, dates from 1959.

'Blue Box' HO/OO W.W.I. 'British Infantry'.

resin manufacturers are strictly outside the remit of this book about classic 'plastic', but his influence in the kit world is significant.

Together with Francois Verlinden and Bob Letterman, two other names, which absolutely must be featured in a list of contemporary military modelling maestros, are Steven Zaloga and Tony Greenland.

Between them, these gentlemen have rewritten the rulebook for the construction of model tanks and armoured fighting vehicles. With an unequalled ability to achieve a true scale effect, Steve and Tony have shown others how to work in etched brass; bending, snapping, braising and soldering side skirts, spaced armour and distressing fenders and gun-shields, from the metal, to achieve super realism. Steven Zaloga is one of those multi-talented modellers, adept in more than one area. He usually accompanies his vehicles with exquisitely painted and animated figures – proving his versatility with both paint and airbrush.

Mention of Mr Zaloga's artistry with figures leads us neatly on to that other military modelling sector – figure modelling.

working with resin, a material that delivered scale accuracy beyond the wildest dreams of modellers, previously used to the limitations of injection-moulded polystyrene.

As more and more modellers opted for the 'Verlinden Way', they sought to emulate his approach. Soon, his artistry was copied and his ever-growing range of products, which had now extended to vehicle and aircraft 'super-detailing' conversion sets, were released to coincide with the new offerings from mainstream giants like Tamiya, Italeri or ESCI. As I mentioned in the introduction, Verlinden kits and those of other

When I realised that models of soldiers could be found other than in boxes of Airfix's 2/- HO/OO soft polythene soldiers, I discovered a whole world of talent that had previously eluded me. The name of Roy Dilley was

½nd scale Vulcan B2 bomber – a Peter Allen classic from 1983

already familiar to me from the pages of *Airfix Magazine*. Roy's versatility revealed to me the dozens of manufacturers who cast 54, 70 (not forgetting 'Series 77') and 90mm model soldiers in lead alloy. Great names such as Hinchcliffe, Imrey-Risley, Mignot, Greenwood & Ball, Hinton Hunt, Tradition, Phoenix, and of course Stadden (Chas Stadden also being an accomplished figure painter). With the growing popularity of model soldiers, it wasn't long before mainstream manufacturers like Airfix, ESCI and Tamiya began making models especially aimed at figure modellers who had traditionally pooh-poohed polystyrene (France's Historex had shown unique faith in 54mm plastic figures since the early 1960s),

Consequently, it wasn't long before kit enthusiasts were encouraged to embellish the offerings of those mainstream manufacturers venturing into the previously haloed ground of military miniatures. And, surprise, surprise, chief amongst these were Airfix, who not only commenced a series of creditable 54mm cavalrymen and foot soldiers but also released numerous boxes of WWII 'Multi-pose' figures (to 54mm or ⅓₂nd scale) which, as their name suggests, were capable of being built into an almost infinite variety of configurations.

Soon, the pages of enthusiast magazines featured the work of modellers like Norman Abbey, Nick Larkin, Sid Horten, Graham Bickerton and Max Longhurst who combined Historex components with those of Airfix or manufacturers of metal figures and created works of bespoke genius.

Together with his ground-breaking work with Poste Militaire, who showed precisely how metal figures should be designed and cast, Ray Lamb also exhibited his mastery with Historex models. As did, of course, artists such as Pierre Conrad and Josaine Desfontaine. No list of military figures is complete without mention of the talents of Peter Gilder, Shep Paine, Ray Anderson, Philip O. Stearns or David Catley, each of whom had an inspirational role in the development of figure modelling.

Today, figure modellers like Mike Blank, Bill Horan, Mike Good, Andrei Koribanics, Peter Twist, Derek Hansen, Adrian Bay and many of those mentioned above are raising the bar even higher – just when most of us had thought that every model-making possibility had been exhausted!

Arguably the biggest single category is aircraft modelling and 'building plastic planes' is anyway how most non-modellers characterise the hobby. Making aircraft models was certainly how I discovered the fun to be had building kits. As a youngster I would rush home from the local toy or model shop – or, if on a trip into town with my parents, the Woolworth's store in the high street – and tear open my new purchase. In those days my chosen model was almost always Airfix, a brand which seemed to be available anywhere. Woolworth's always carried virtually the entire range, a legacy of a close commercial relationship dating back to the 1940s. If I fancied a change, I was

FROG catalogue (1960s).

Magnificent ¼th scale BAe Sea Harrier FRS-1

confident that the nearest newsagent would also stock FROG kits – brand owner Lines Brothers having explored all channels to circumnavigate Airfix's apparent retail monopoly.

Initially my purchases were assembled and painted at a frantic rate. Undercarriage legs and tail planes would frequently wobble and lean precariously before falling off the model dripping in strings of pungently sticky polystyrene cement. Dissatisfied with my crude and hurried attempts, I would invariably consign my recent purchase to target practice with an air rifle or the hungry lick of a flaming match. Didn't plastic fighters and bombers burn well then?

As my abilities improved I discovered that Humbrol's old marketing strap line of "Skill and patience ..." really did pay dividends. As I took more care, my finished models began to pay more than a passing resemblance to the aircraft they were supposed to mimic.

It wasn't long before I heeded the advice of experts such as Alan Hall, Michael Bowyer and Chris Ellis, learning the importance of accurate camouflage colours and discovering how to cement crystal-clear cockpit transparencies to fuselages without causing them to mist up from the effects of polystyrene cement dissolving adjacent plastic.

One of the biggest influences on me in my twenties was Ray Rimmel, the aviation buff who seemed to contribute to every modelling magazine and actually became Airfix Magazine's editor for a while.

An expert on WWI avia-

tion, Ray now runs the perennially successful Windsock imprint and, as far as I know, still employs the talents of one-time Airfix artist, Brian Knight, to illustrate the covers of successive volumes.

After a while I became aware of the amazing talents of master aircraft modellers such as George Lee, Peter Cooke and Alan Clarke. These gentlemen showed precisely what could be achieved by scratch-building, although, if I'm honest, their dexterity with metal work and bespoke vacuum forming was always beyond me.

More recently I became aware of some of the work of Bill Bosworth (see Accurate Miniatures) and had the distinct pleasure of meeting someone who had turned his passion into a career.

At the time of writing I have just become aware of the model creations of Zdenek Sebesta – now one of Europe's foremost aircraft modellers whose work has recently been exhibited in print.

Like military modelling, the field of aircraft modelling appears to offer unlimited potential. These opportunities are no doubt greatly aided by the huge range of after-market tools, accessories and conversion packs which enable the keen modeller to achieve near 100 per cent scale accuracy. With the application of photo-etched seat harnesses and tiny cockpit instruments reproduced as decals and then sandwiched behind ultra-thin transparent plastic and etched brass bezels, the realism achieved by some 21st-century modellers would astound pioneers like James Hay Stevens.

Though never a model railway enthusiast, I would occasionally buy one of Airfix's 'Line-side' kits. These were usually of either buildings or trackside accessories like fences or telegraph poles. Though scaled to HO/OO (which is really ⅟₇₆th scale) they were ideal accompaniments for dioramas in the more common ⅟₇₂nd scale. Indeed Airfix re-branded their RAF Control Tower, originally a railway layout accessory in HO/OO, as a ⅟₇₂nd scale airfield accessory designed for display with the firm's enormous range of ⅟₇₂nd scale RAF aircraft. No one seemed to notice the

Addar 'Planet of the Apes Treehouse' in ... a bottle! (1975) Established by ex-Aurora employees, Addar began life in 1972 and released lots of ships in bottles too. They were mostly ex-Gowland & Gowland or Aurora moulds. Sadly, the company ceased trading in 1977.

discrepancy in size.

Whilst I was never lured by the appeal of the working model trains of Hornby, Marklin, Fleischmann or Arnold – and reserved my modelling mainly to military vehicles and aircraft – I did keep a weather-eye on the work of modellers like Michael Andress and Bert Lamkin. These enthusiasts used the products of Airfix, Faller and Merit (with enormous dexterity) plus a range of craft material, to design and populate layouts of the most intricate complexity.

Like model railways, car kits never really caught my attention. Occasionally of course, one of Airfix's more ambitious models, notably Peter Allen's magnificent ½th scale 'Bentley Blower', would tease hard-earned cash from my pocket. I was also sometimes tempted to purchase one of Revell's outrageous street machines. I remember buying their outlandish 'Street L'eagle' trike in 1972. Of course, today I wish I had purchased one or two of Revell's early car kits and especially some of 'Big Daddy' Ed Roth's customised creations. Look at the values these achieve today!

Two of the biggest names in car modelling were Gerald Scarborough and Mat Irvine – the latter produced regular articles about what was new and exciting in the world of car kits.

Mat is also well known for his love of space and

science fiction models and thus we neatly segue into the final major genre in the plastic construction kit world – space and sci-fi.

Mat Irvine will need little introduction to British modellers. During a reception for model collectors and car enthusiasts at Dean Milano's excellent Chicago Toy and Model Museum in September 2003, I had the chance to interview briefly fellow Brit Mat who, during one of his regular visits to the 'states, was staying with Dean.

In fact Mat and I had met before. At the 2002 British IPMS extravaganza at Telford, we exchanged our latest books: Mat's *Creating Space*, an illustrated history of space kits, and my work, *Celebration of Flight* – the illustrated history of Roy Cross's career in aviation art which I co-authored with the artist. Coincidentally we were both in attendance signing our respective works for those kind souls ready to part with their hard-earned!

At the Chicago party I was able to ask Mat about his long involvement with model kits.

June 1990 a collecting special from *Scale Models* magazine.

Denys Fisher 'Six Million Dollar Man' kit.

Tony James' Comet Miniatures ⅛th scale 'Mk1 TV Dalek'.

"As a youngster, I started buying 'two bob' Airfix kits from Woolworth's, spreading glue all over the kitchen table much to Mum's disgust," he said. Later as he entered his teens, although he discovered the charms of cars and girls (not necessarily in that order) he decided not to abandon modelling.

After he left school he joined the BBC, not initially in SFX, which is his current metier, but in the newsroom. "It was the time of Apollo 11 and although BBC 2 was broadcasting in colour, and BBC 1 was about to embrace the new medium, there was a lack of original colour film to broadcast," he said. Being a keen modeller and basically using Airfix kits and assorted bits and pieces, new boy Mat was able to put his hobby talents to good use and furnished 'Auntie Beeb' with a range of three-dimensional replicas, in colour of course, which proved

MPC's snap-together 'The Bionic Woman' repair laboratory.

a very valuable supplement to the broadcaster's programmes.

"It was a very crude set-up by today's standard," smiled Mat, "but it was all achieved very quickly. Remember, the whole thing had to be done within 24 hours. There was no time to waste." It was these early experiences of model making which encouraged Mat's abiding love of space travel and exploration. It also taught him the rigours of working under pressure, within a tight schedule and to a budget. Invaluable lessons for a features contributor in the unforgiving world of specialist publications.

At around the time Mat was producing his space models for BBC news, he developed his interest in American cars. "I have to admit a fondness for American machinery – mainly as these were the first

model cars to be made in the larger scales," he told me.

"At this time Airfix car kits, nice as they were, were manufactured in ½nd scale, which was smaller than American kits (generally in ¼th scale). Neither did they have rubber tyres or lots of chrome parts which were desirable features common to American kits."

Mat distinctly remembers encountering an impressive AMT kit of a 1962 Ford 'Fairlane', which was bigger and more impressive than anything he had seen in England. "In those days, if you wanted to build larger kits you had to opt for American models by AMT, Revell or Monogram," he recalled.

"Although I sometimes make aircraft kits, a long time ago I realised I had to specialise," he said. With experience of model making for TV under his belt, Mat soon transferred to the BBC effects department – usually working in the Space Studio. He worked on a wide vari-ety of programmes from Apollo, Soyuz and Skylab to unmanned missions like Mariner and Viking. Although his interest in models and specifically cars started as a hobby, it is ironic that Mat's long association with space started as part of his job.

As a BBC Visual Effects Designer, Mat is most famous for his creations on programmes such as 'Doctor Who', 'Blake's 7' and 'Tomorrow's World'. Working to an extremely tight budget and without the luxury of the sophisticated CGI techniques made famous today by Lucas Films and Pixar, Mat and his team had to think on their feet and be ready to assemble whatever the story required. "You get the script and then you basi-cally have to work out what is likely to be either a model or creature effect," he added.

AMT Star Trek (early version) *USS Enterprise.*

Airfix Series 10 'Snowspeeder' from 'The Empire Strikes Back'.

Pretty collectible Denys Fisher 'R2-D2' kit (1978).

Airfix 'Slave I' from 'The Empire Strikes Back'.

Mat left the BBC in 1993 and afterwards helped start the American import 'Robot Wars' in the UK. He was one of the main Technical Consultants on the first few series. Now he's now involved with the judging panel.

Together with his former regular monthly feature in *Scale Models International*, Mat has had many pieces published for journals that include *Airfix Magazine*, *Model Cars Plus*, *Model and Collectors Mart*, *Tamiya Model Magazine*, America's *Fine Scale Modeler* and even Britain's *New Scientist*. He is also a regular contributor to myriad sci-fi and car magazines. Although recognised as an expert about the history and development of plastic kits, he is not precious about kit collecting *per se*, preferring to see assembled models professionally displayed, rather than unassembled gathering dust in attic hoards. "It depends what you mean by collectible," he told me. "You can have a collection of boxes if you particularly covet the artwork."

His ambivalence to kits as investments might have something to do with his matter-of-fact relationship with them whilst preparing articles for specialist magazines or in advance of seeing them destroyed on a film set. He told me that he was forced

Lincoln's 'FAB 1' car from TV's 'Thunderbirds'.

to construct kits at such a furious rate, people were amazed that he could finish and photograph them so rapidly. But, as he says, he is in control of the actual image, "so if I screwed up one side of a model I would simply photograph it from the opposite side!"

In 'Creating Space', Mat says: "Not that long ago, second-hand kits were not worth more than a fraction of their retail price – and in fact most still are not. Like the majority of objects now deemed 'collectible', just because they are old (or perhaps to be more accurate, 'not brand new'), this doesn't mean that they are worth anything more than a second-hand price, and certainly no more than face value." However, even Mat has to concede that there are exceptions and that some old kits are worth their weight in gold. He cited rarities such as American manufacturer Hawk's 'Martin Matador' missile on its transporter and Lindberg's 'Five Space Ships of the Future' set, both from the 1950s, as eminently desirable finds for collectors.

Tony James needs little introduction to space and science fiction modellers. His Lavender Hill shop, Comet Models, is a Mecca for those visiting London, keen to discover the latest kit or collectible associated with science fiction or man's exploration of space. However, I first met Tony many years ago when he dealt in old and rare kits from much smaller premises nearby. This operation, 'Tee-Jay

Models', was launched in 1986 after Tony attended the Biggin Hill Air Fair.

"I took along my collection to sell and returned on the Sunday with three times as many kits, a van and £3,000," Tony told me. "All weekend I was offered second-hand kits including many out-of-production types, so I decided to start a business specialising in these and other hard-to-find kits."

Incidentally, Tony recently told me that as far as nostalgia is concerned "time plays many tricks. Who ever thought the three-colour 'trench panel' kits from Matchbox would become collectible!"

Initially, Tony's new business, situated in one room under the present shop, was open by appointment only. "One of our Japanese customers offered some 'Thunderbirds' kits in exchange for some stock. This highlighted a gap in the market and I immediately began to offer Science Fiction kits as part of the business."

As things developed, Tony launched Comet Miniatures in 1989 and since then it has expanded on the same site. "We produced our first model (CM001) which was a vacform and white metal kit of the 'Nautilus Submarine' from '20,000 Leagues Under The Sea' and followed this with models of 'Stingray' and 'Fireball XL5'," he continued. "We then launched this country's first plastic kits of the TV and movie version 'Daleks'. Our final in-house model was the 'Blake's Seven' spaceship, 'Liberator'. All these kits are now discontinued and have since become sought-after collectors' pieces."

Readers might be interested to learn that before branching out on his own, Tony was an RAF Air Traffic Controller. Significantly, he spent his last five years with the RAF as a model maker. "I was lucky to be involved with a specialist team building full-size replica aircraft – 'Hawks', including a Red Arrows version, and a 'Tornado'," he recalled. Tony's specialist area was painting cockpit instrumentation and finishing the pilot's 'office'.

Now 54 years of age, Tony tells me he built his very first model at the age of five. "It was an Airfix

'Skyhawk'! Airfix and FROG set the standards for other manufacturers to follow and it is a sad reflection to have to look to foreign companies for the future of our hobby," Tony reflected. "I will always remember that it was the exciting artwork on the box tops which set our imaginations racing and had us running home from Woolworth's with our latest purchase only to get scolded by Mum for leaving glue and paint stains on the kitchen table! Today's PC rules have removed part of the fun from the hobby and no matter how good the kit is, it is the artwork which sets the expectation of the contents."

Comet Miniatures now specialises in Limited Edition Resin Sci-Fi kits as well as Die-Casts. "I still have the enthusiasm and will continue to produce items that enthusiasts require and it is a pleasing thought that the RAF Museum at Hendon still has three of my models on permanent display," Tony concluded.

I can't really end this section without mention of ship modelling. Lots of modellers specialise in this area. Two who had an enormous influence on me were Chris Ellis and Roger Chesnau.

Every manufacturer has a number of either warships or civilian vessels in their ranges. Choice is pretty neatly polarised between those who favour ships from the age of sail and those preferring armoured, steel battleships, etc., from the 20th century. With the latter, scales vary from Tamiya's substantial $\frac{1}{350}$th scale mammoths to $\frac{1}{1,200}$th scale waterline vessels, popular with war gamers and also made in plastic, in 'waterline' versions, first by Eaglewall in the 1950s and by Airfix in the 1970s – in Britain at least.

Scale Models magazine, November 1992.

4. Kit Collecting

The Model Village – one of the dozens of wartime publications showing youngsters how to build models from scrap card and paper.

Like the models they covet, kit collectors come in all shapes and sizes. Some scale model enthusiasts buy kits purely to construct, perfecting authentic details in every way and then displaying them in the hope of receiving the plaudits of their peers. Others seek out long-lost kits lurking in the dustier recesses of retail stores or amidst the debris of jumble in a relative's loft. But whatever their game plan – to build or hoard for potential future investment – model fans like me regularly scour locations we think might reveal hidden gems from modelling's history.

Of course it doesn't really matter why we 'anoraks' search out discontinued kits. It's a harmless pursuit and as long as it brings some per-

sonal satisfaction and isn't inconveniencing anyone, it's as valid as any hobby. When I began to collect kits, shortly after I learnt of the possible demise of Airfix in 1981, I rather grandiosely thought that by collecting a few examples of their products, which I had so eagerly built in the 1960s, I was preserving an important part of our social history. Certainly, I began collecting old kits because they were affordable – even 20 years ago rare Dinky cars or Britain's lead soldiers were beyond my price range. Old kits were cheap. I also figured that because they were relatively inexpensive when originally retailed and they lacked any perceived financial worth, most models must have ended up in the bin. I figured that ironically, this would mean that unmade kits, in their original packaging, would consequently be quite rare and that maybe, just maybe, they would be a long-term investment which 'serious' collectors had overlooked.

Well, prices for old models have sky-rocketed since I wrote my first book about kit collecting (1984's *Model World of Airfix*) and the phrase 'no-pain, no-gain' certainly has a resonance with kit collectors. You could buy a second-hand car for the price of some of the scarcer FROG, Airfix or Aurora kits!

Commercial opportunity in the kit-collecting world has made it possible for some people to dedicate part or all of their time to trading in collectable kits. But, before we consider one or two collectors and their activities, I thought it worthwhile singling out a few traders, two from the UK one from the US, so that we can better understand the current passion for old kits and, especially, the price we are prepared to pay for the long-lost models that we can't do without.

Malcolm Rolling started Shropshire-based 'KingKit' from his spare bedroom in 1983. Then, he was turning

FROG Penguin 'DH 86A Diana' (1930s).

over some £50 per week. He decided to trade in old and discontinued kits after he discovered that his interests had changed and he thought of selling his personal model collection. Fortunately, this decision coincided with the temporary demise of Airfix, which suddenly put a premium on the examples of their kits he had earmarked for sale.

After maintaining the business on a strictly part-time basis, in 1989 with the annual turnover growing to £20,000, Malcolm decided to bite the bullet and trade in kits full-time. His decision was encouraged when he discovered his children using parcels he had painstakingly packed full of fragile old kits, as the building blocks for a western fort playing cowboys and indians around the 'redoubt'.

Realising that he had reached a fork in the road – the business was too serious to run part time from home – and wanting to change direction anyway, he secured a 3,000-square foot warehouse and went full-time.

"It was a difficult decision but on the basis that you don't regret what you do in life, you regret what you don't do, I decided to give it a go," he said.

Fortunately, Malcolm has experienced a boom in the interest of old kits – which has not surprisingly coincided with the rapid decline of new kits appearing in the shops as manufacturers reduce production and concentrate on fewer new kits. Since it began, KingKit has become one of the largest old and rare kit traders in the business, now with an annual turnover of more than £250,000. KingKit stocks more than 100,000 kits and publishes a quarterly catalogue that has become an accepted 'value guide' to collectors everywhere.

Malcolm was keen that I understood all the type designation collectors use to distinguish earlier types of Airfix packaging from more recent ones. For example, the first types of bagged kit header are designated 'Type 1' and so on. "The Airfix Type designations ... how they came about," he began. "When I started in 1983 I got a letter from a Brian Bunce of Norwich who sent me a photocopied hand-drawn diagram of the various Airfix bag tops designating them type I, II and III. He was a novelty then – a collector of Airfix kits. These designations seemed so logical I took them up too and now everyone uses them. I think it's time he got recognition," Malcolm urged.

Malcolm also told me he could never understand why the Airfix blister packs aren't really collected. "You can see that all the kit is there and hasn't been opened or tampered with," he

Box Brownie snaps taken by a teenage modeller during wartime. The threads supporting the 'Heinkel' are almost invisible!

FROG advertisement (1930s).

Blister-packed 'MiG-15' from 1973 (kit dates to 1958).

said, bemused why they never feature in dealers' lists. I reckon that the very fact that this award-winning packaging, introduced by Airfix in 1973, required ripping off the vacuum-formed clear blister from its card header to inspect the moulded pieces, means that few remain intact. Consequently, in the decade before the advent of 'collectors' shows on TV, few thought about saving the cheaper products and I'm sure most of them were inadvertently damaged and therefore unsuitable for second-hand sale. Collectors know that bagged headers could be carefully separated from the poly bag containing the Airfix kit and could then stealthily be re-stapled. Boxed kits, on the other hand, simply required the sellotape securing lid to base to be cut with a sharp knife – without any damage to the overall presentation. Blister packed kits didn't stand a chance. So, they must be scarce. Right?

"The market has changed over the 20 years I have been in kits," said Malcolm. "There are now endless kit re-issues and whereas the price on a discontinued item used to be created by the builders, now they can be set by the collectors.

"I haven't got a favourite kit, but I especially like the box art I remember from when I was a child. Airfix 'Type 3' (dating from the late-1960s to very early-1970s, the

Two versions of the Beam Engine originating in 1966.

last type of packaging sporting the remnant of Airfix's original 'banner' logotype) brings back happy memories. I remember popping into the local model shop in Falmouth and seeing they had the new 'RAF Emergency Set' in stock – but I didn't have enough cash on me. I dashed home and got more money, but the shop had sold out by the time I got back. The next delivery wasn't until the following month … an eternity for a 12 year old to wait!"

You see readers? Memories are made of this!

I first encountered the activities of Pat Lewarne in 1987 when I purchased his excellent *Enthusiasts Guide to Airfix Models*. Since then I have bought kits from his firm 'Collectakit' by mail order and on odd occasions from Collectakit stands at hobby fairs. Together with Malcolm Rollings' KingKit, Collectakit has more or less cornered the British second-hand kit market, offering a reliable and reasonably priced service to enthusiasts in desperate need for that long discontinued model.

"Many modellers view the collecting of un-built kits as a sad hobby worthy of anoraks," Pat told me. "However the majority of modellers will be the first to admit to purchasing more models than they can build. This over-purchasing varies from 20-plus 'in stock', to thousands in the loft. Surplus stock or collections, whatever you prefer to call them, of several hundred models are quite common. So why would anyone initially buy extra kits

Original Saunders-Roe 'S-R53' header, 1958.

– perhaps there was an offer at the model shop, perhaps the kit has been superseded by a better one or perhaps the modeller's tastes have changed. The latter has been the beginning of many a collection."

I asked Pat to expand on other reasons that encouraged kit collecting. "A second key driver is nostalgia," he answered. "Many models are still purchased on the basis of 'this was the first kit I built'. Most people will then want further examples of kits from that era of their life. Some people will be really selective about what they collect, whilst others will splurge and buy anything. The latter will normally be the shorter-term collector, returning their collection to the market within ten years. Others will be drawn into trading unwanted extra items either at shows or on line.

"The final category is the 'build it when

Airfix ¹⁄₇₂nd scale Boomerang fighter, 1965.

Just like the real thing!

Airfix kits are not just models—they're exact replicas, each series to a constant scale.

There are models galore in the Airfix range! Aircraft from fighters to bombers (all to the same 1/72nd scale), 00 gauge railway accessories, vintage cars, warships. Airfix value is unbeatable— ask your dealer for the latest list.

Nearly 100 kits from 2/- to 10/6.

AIRFIX
THE WORLD'S GREATEST VALUE IN CONSTRUCTION KITS
From Model and Hobby Shops, Toy Shops and F. W. Woolworth

Airfix press ads from the mid-1960s.

The classic ships of history!

Full-page advertisement for FROG flying and non-flying (Penguin) kits in a pre-war edition of *Meccano Magazine*.

THE MECCANO MAGAZINE

FROG FLYING MODEL KITS—YOU CAN BUILD AND FLY THESE
No tools needed—all parts cut to shape

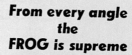
HAWKER HURRICANE 2/-   HAWKER DEMON 4/6

AVENGER 1/-

From every angle the FROG is supreme

Every FROG model combines excellent appearance and design with accurate construction, while the flying models have an unequalled performance.

Whether scale or non-scale, flying or non-flying, ready-made or in kit form— each FROG model is supreme in its class. FROG ready to fly models are obtainable from 1/- to 42/-, flying construction kits from 1/6 to 21/- and Penguin non-flying scale models from 3/- to 21/-.

A new branch of the famous FROG Service is the introduction of comprehensive kits of material, including Balsa wood, fully-shaped airscrews, etc., details of which can be obtained from your local FROG stockist.

Many more models to choose from, including competition models to S.M.A.E. specification. See them at your local toyshop or fill in and post coupon below for the new FROG catalogue.

MAIL PLANE 10/6

SILVER ARROW 2/6

PV6 DIVE BOMBER 6/6

PERCIVAL GULL KIT 3/- MADE UP 5/-

FAIREY BATTLE KIT 5/- MADE UP 8/6

DE HAVILLAND DIANA KIT 7/6 MADE UP 15/-

ROTA AUTOGIRO KIT 3/6 MADE UP 6/6

VICKERS WELLESLEY KIT 7/6 MADE UP 15/-

FROG MODEL AIRCRAFT
Covered by World Patents granted and pending. Made in England by International Model Aircraft Ltd.
OBTAINABLE AT ALL GOOD TOYSHOPS AND STORES Sole Concessionaires:
LINES BROS. LTD., MORDEN ROAD, MERTON, S.W.19

COUPON   *Please send me your "Frog" coloured leaflet with particulars of the "Frog" Flying Club and how to obtain handsome enamelled "Frog" Pilot badges.*
To Lines Bros. Ltd. (Dept. 5), Morden Road, London, S.W.19
NAME..............................
ADDRESS..............................

FROG advertisement in *Meccano Magazine*, 1938.

THE MECCANO MAGAZINE

VICKERS WELLESLEY CONSTRUCTION KIT 2'6

...EAKERS

The Vickers Wellesley came into public favour by its wonderful Egypt-Australia non-stop flight.

Frog Aeroplanes have always been favourites of the air-minded youth of Britain. The new FROG model of the record-breaking Vickers Wellesley is perhaps the most interesting of the FROG range of inexpensive constructor kits. It will give hours of pleasure to any amateur constructor, and, when it is completed, it really does fly.

Constructor kits from 1/6 to 2/-, including models to S.M.A.E. competition specifications.

USE THE BEST MATERIALS

Promising models sometimes give disappointing results, not because of errors in design, but through the use of inferior materials and inefficient airscrews. Do not make this mistake when building your new machine.
International Model Aircraft Ltd, so long famous for the excellent workmanship of the FROG models, are now supplying balsa wood, tissue, fully shaped airscrews and everything needed by the model aeroplane maker. These materials are of the same high standard as used in FROG S.M.A.E. Competition Models. Ask for them by name at your local FROG stockists.

ALWAYS ASK FOR   **FROG** SERVICE IS ALWAYS AT YOUR SERVICE

FROG AERO SUPPLIES
Covered by World Patents granted and pending. Made in England by International Model Aircraft Ltd.
OBTAINABLE AT ALL GOOD DEALERS AND STORES. Sole Concessionaires:
LINES BROS. LTD., MORDEN RD., MERTON, S.W.19

COUPON   To Lines Bros. Ltd. (Dept. 5), Morden Road, London S.W.19
NAME..............................
ADDRESS..............................

JUST LIKE THE REAL THING!

The magnificent V.C.10. This authentic 1/144 scale model of the powerful jet liner now in use with the leading air lines, is made from a superbly detailed 74 part kit costing 6/-. It's one of many exciting kits by Airfix. There are over 200 of them, covering 13 different series. And at 2/- to 17/6 you can well afford to make all your models *just like the real thing.*

STOP PRESS: WILDCAT VI

AIRFIX CONSTANT SCALE
CONSTRUCTION KITS
Just like the real thing!
From model and hobby shops, toy shops and F. W. Woolworth

ALL THAT'S NEW IN MODELLING!
Airfix Catalogue 9d. and Monthly Magazine 1/6.

'Just Like The Real Thing!' advertisement in *Airfix Magazine* from 1964.

I retire' collector. This individual stores up large numbers of kits to build in a yet-to-be-achieved retirement. Whilst some do achieve this, many change their minds after filling the loft, or sadly do not make it to retirement."

However, like me, Pat recognises that there are often simpler, more emotionally subjective reasons for hunting down long-obsolete kits. "What all these people have in common, whether they regard themselves as modellers or collectors, is pleasure in owning the item," he said.

"Nowadays there are many kits that you would not build because that model has been replaced by a better one. In many of these cases, it is the box artwork that attracts the collector. Few people will dispute the fact that modern box art is inferior to older box art. Comparison of a Georgian carriage clock to a modern digital alarm clock springs to mind."

I asked Pat how he thought newcomers to kit collecting should begin. "Firstly do you have 'stock' in your loft? Is that what you want to expand on or can you use them for part exchange? Try to find old catalogues or reference books. Get sales lists from specialist second-hand kit dealers to find out what is available and at what prices. Do not get drawn into online or auction sales at this time – you do not yet have enough knowledge. Other sources that you can sample are car boot sales, toy fairs and specialist Kit Shows (mainly IPMS). Always bear in mind, the rarer the kit, the longer you may have to look for it.

"People will ask 'what should I collect?'" he continued. "Provided you are not collecting just to make money, it should be something that pleases you. It could be aircraft, airliners, vehicles, figures, ships or sci-fi, etc. Only the collector can determine what he wants to collect, but it is sometimes useful to find out what is available and how readily it can be obtained."

So how did Pat become a 'specialist kit dealer'? "As the quantity of kits coming on to the market as second-hand items increased beyond what the traditional model shop could handle, so specialists sprang up. Some can trace their history to meeting the market,

Matchbox kit catalogue, 1974/75.

whilst others had been long-term collectors and this was the next stage for them. Collectakit, based in Surrey, can trace its roots back to the 1950s, building Airfix tractors, aircraft, and tanks."

Pat had a 'major involvement' with model railways in the 1970s and then switched back to kits 20 years ago, which resulted in the emergence of Collectakit. Initially he focused on the ready market at Toy Shows, and then quickly followed this with a mail-order service. A natural development was Collectakit's subsequent attendance at IPMS (International Plastic Modellers Society) shows around the UK.

Pat told me that today Collectakit could be called a 'kit recycler'. With a smile he added that this gives it 'green' credentials: "Because not only is it a source of old kits, but it also repatriates quantities of relatively recent kits."

So how does someone like Collectakit price kits?

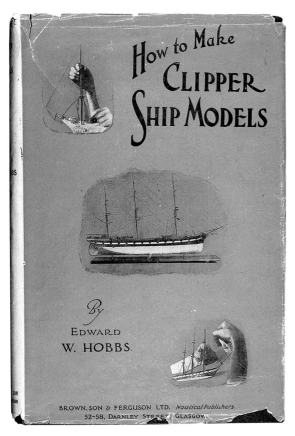

'How to make Clipper Ship Models', 1940s.

"Well of course it is based on the purchase price but also on availability. Something that only appears every five years is going to be more desirable than something that appears every day. The 'wants' of collectors are always a good barometer of demand – although this can change every time a specialist magazine prints an article on certain kits. Always beware the collector who says 'I remember those at 2/6 in Woolies' – cause that's all he wants to pay!"

Pat tells me that his favourite items are old gift sets. "Why gift sets? Well, mostly they were fairly short run productions, in specialist packing. These are not your modern gift sets – any three kits in a uniform sleeve – but kits that have been repackaged, usually in a unique box for a specific purpose. This could vary from Christmas to an historic event." Because there are fewer gift sets than single kits issued, Pat told me that their rarity naturally adds to their collectors' value. Now there's a tip.

Revell-Monogram's Ed Sexton introduced me to Paul Milam, proprietor of the eponymous US kit dealership. Since then, I have added Milam Models to my small roster of reliable rare-kit suppliers. Indeed, some of the models shown on the pages of this book were bought from Paul.

"I began building plastic model kits when I was six years old," he told me. "I would put them together and my older sister would paint the wing or prop tips. As I recall these were Aurora kits. I have been in love with modelling ever since. From my earliest memories all I wanted to be was a fighter pilot, and modelling all of those hot jets of the early 1950s only strengthened that desire. As it turned out, my less than perfect eyesight prevented my being the next Steve Canon (an American comic hero – Aurora produced a kit of him in full flight gear standing in front of an 'F-102A'). But I did learn to fly and spent the next 40 years as a professional pilot.

"About 22 years ago I was introduced to John Burns' Kit Collector group. I have been a member since. The KCC (Kit Collectors Clearinghouse – see p. 181) opened a

1910 'B Type' Bus, 1966.

BRONCO

1/72 SCALE Unassembled Model Kit
Molded in Color
AGES 8 Years thru Adult

Photos of Actual Model

US Airfix 'Bronco'.

Quarter scale Aurora 'SNJ' trainer.

SNJ *TRAINER* ¼" SCALE MODEL

.69

FAMOUS FIGHTERS TRADE MARK

By *Aurora*

ALL PLASTIC ASSEMBLY KIT

MADE IN ENGLAND   PATTERN No. 1384

AIRFIX

SCALE MODEL

MESSERSCHMITT
Me 109 F
CONSTRUCTION KIT
HIGH IMPACT MATERIAL

INCLUDING DISPLAY STAND

OF THE AIRFIX SERIES OF SCALE MODELS OF FAMOUS TYPES OF AIRCRAFT

Original 'Me109F' from 1956.

FLYING WHITEHOUSE
E-4 BOEING 747

UNITED STATES OF AMERICA

1/14 4 Scale-Unassembled Model Kit
Modèle Reduit Pour Assembler

Featuring SCALE-MASTER

US-Airfix

USAirfix ¹⁄₁₄₄th scale, Boeing 747 'Flying Whitehouse' based on the 1969 original.

AIRFIX-72 SCALE
FOLLAND GNAT

Folland 'Gnat', 1964.

whole new world to me - there were modellers looking for old and out-of-production kits, and willing to pay a handsome price."

At that time Paul had a small collection of maybe 400 kits: "Some of which were old and collectors' items, but I was not a collector. I was going to build every one of them," he added.

"Almost everyone that builds models has the same story. We all become collectors by default, buying far more kits than we can ever build. So I too am a collector. But that's good because you can't have too many kits.

"I accepted a position as a pilot flying for a major retailer and that took me to all 50 states and several countries. Every time I flew to a new city I would visit all of the hobby shops and toy stores, time permitting, looking for out-of-production kits. It was amazing how many I found. The profit paid for my hobby and then some," he recalled.

Paul soon had 1,000 kits, then 2,000, then 4,000. "Today the inventory is around 12,000," he said. "Becoming a business was an easy decision, and I have never looked back, this being my 20th year. We sell kits and a limited selection of decals and books worldwide. We publish five or six sales flyers per year and attend 10

to 15 model contests, shows or conventions per year."

Paul retired from commercial flying almost two years ago and now devotes all his time to the Milam Model business.

I asked Paul what collectors look for. "As to what is the most collectable kit? I don't think that there is a single kit at the top of most collectors' want list," he answered. "Having said that, I would put the ITC 'XF-108' kit in the top group, because it was only issued once and never will be again, and it is a kit of an aircraft that never was. North American Aviation did produce a wooden mock-up of the 'F-108' but the kit was almost a totally different aircraft, being launched like a 'Nike' missile. Others at the top of the list are first issues of many Aurora aircraft, such as their 'Me-109', 'P-40', 'B-29', 'B-25', 'Fw-190' and 'Zero'.

"I still get excited when a new kit comes out that I want to build and I am currently working on two. A dear friend in Seattle is building a paint booth for me, something I have wanted and needed for a long time. Now I should be able to complete my models with a better paint finish." As most readers will know, a paint, or spray, booth is invaluable for preventing surplus paint from an airbrush ruining adjacent furniture or fabrics!

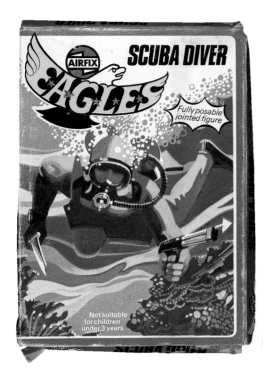

Airfix '*Eagles*' Adventure sets and individual figures – eminently collectable.

"I have always found modelling a relaxing pastime, an education on the history of aviation, people and places. I am convinced that modelling helped prepare me for my career as a pilot and helped me relax after a long day in the office at 43,000 feet. Fortunately I have been lucky enough to meet many who share my belief – that model miniatures are a satisfying and satisfactory way to spend what little free time we have today, enabling the curious to understand technological developments and milestones in aviation or military history in a way that studying archive footage or, worse still, the products of Hollywood studios can never do." Hear hear, Paul.

Where can you contact people like Milam Models, Collectakit and KingKit? Mostly they advertise in specialist modeling magazines or within the pages of newsletters published by enthusiasts groups such as the IPMS and Kit Collectors Clearinghouse. They have web sites and they appear at shows. Many will supply printed sales lists or email copies. Try to come to model shows and see the array of kits available and talk to like-minded people. The one common denominator amongst all those involved on the periphery of the plastic model industry is a love and interest in the history and development of plastic construction kits. You'll be amazed at what you might learn!

There isn't space here to mention all the enthusiastic

Ford '3 litre G.T.', 1969.

modellers and collectors that I have met and got to like. Anyway, many readers will know the likes of John Wells, Graham Short, Trevor Snowden, Anthony Lawrence, Bill Bosworth and Mark Stevens.

However, I feel that it's worthwhile singling out one or two enthusiasts with whom I have got more closely acquainted during the preparation of this book.

I asked Jeremy Brook, secretary of the Airfix Collectors' Club and publishing editor of its newsletter *Constant Scale,* about his particular passion for Airfix and how he finds the time to produce a regular, illustrated newsletter.

"I first started buying Airfix kits in the late 50s and had a racing set for Christmas shortly after it was first released. In 1963, when I was 13, I started buying *Airfix Magazine* and the catalogues, as well as collecting every leaflet or price list that came out. I had developed a strong interest for all things Airfix, although the kits always were my first love. Much as I enjoyed making models and playing with my hugely expanded racing set, I was probably more interested in the development of the ranges, the packaging and artwork, etc. With the brilliant Roy Cross and Brian Knight artwork and the logical development of the various ranges, Airfix seemed far ahead of its then competitors. During the 70s I kept careful records of all the kit releases, which has stood me in good stead when I took over the mantle of running the Airfix Collectors' Club.

"Following Airfix's bankruptcy in 1981, I lost some interest as it was no longer the 'Airfix' I'd known and was passionate about. Then, in the late 90s I joined FAMAS (the club dedicated to FROG and Airfix) and the Airfix Collectors' Club and was delighted to find that there were clubs and organisations that were devoted to the study of Airfix.

"Having written some articles for the Club magazine *Constant Scale*, things went quiet! One day I 'phoned up the founder of the club, John Wells, who informed me that he was inundated with work and asked would I like to take on the running of the club. I couldn't refuse! So I produced a magazine and sent it out to all the existing

'HP 0/400', 1968.

'Craft Master' (USA)
version of Airfix
'Fairey Swordfish'.

¹⁄₉₆th scale Triang Air
France 'Caravelle'.

members, most of whom rejoined and were delighted that the club was active again.

"I now produce four magazines a year as well as a calendar, both of which are now commercially printed and include colour on a regular basis. Club members such as Arthur Ward supply me with articles and photographs; the remaining content comes from my records and collection. With well over 600 models produced by Airfix over the last 50 years, I should have more than enough information to keep going for the next 150 years or so!"

Airfix 'Dragster' originating from MPC in the United States.

The author of this book has a special reason for being grateful for Jeremy's efforts. Together with continuing my 'honorary membership' of the club, originally conferred on me by the inimitable John Wells, Jeremy has also revived my *nom de plume* from the old *Airfix Magazine* days and now as 'Tailgunner Ward' of old, I write occasional articles for *Constant Scale*!

Long-time Airfix fan David James runs one of the best enthusiasts' websites available. Certainly, if you want to better understand the variations in packaging or learn more about some of the British firm's earliest releases in construction kits, games or toy, his site is a must.

Married with four children (home is in Hampshire), David is an IT manager for IBM. Working from offices in Belgium he runs their project management education organisation for Europe.

David tells me he has been "mad about kits from the earliest age", and has made literally hundreds, mostly Airfix. He remembers that he used to cycle to Woolworth's every week to get another one. "Now, how many times must you have heard that! What would we have done without 'Woolies'?"

David, who was born in Bristol, tells me

that his favourite model shop was in nearby Weston-Super-Mare. "Whenever my parents took us to the seaside I always used to drag them to this shop just to look in the window ... full of unobtainable American Monogram and Lindberg kits which being larger scale than Airfix or FROG always appeared massive and mouth-watering."

He doesn't remember his first kit but recalls with amusement taking an Airfix kit to 'show and tell' at the end of term at junior school. "I took in the 'SRN-1' hovercraft to make. In my normal manner I couldn't be bothered to wait for the glue to dry so it wouldn't stand on its little wheels!

"I started as a modeller – a fanatic," he said. "I think that as a teenage boy I must have purchased and assembled nearly the whole Airfix range, plus many more from FROG and Revell. I still make the occasional model, but in adulthood my desire for modelling perfection far outstrips my abilities."

So why start collecting?

"For me the reason was that I saved most of the instruction sheets from the models that I made. Why? I have no idea! I just kept them. As I grew up, married, moved house several times, my

1970s Fantasy Kits.

cherished box of kit instruction sheets came with me. Then, a couple of years ago, I opened this box and realised two things – firstly that some of what I was looking at was old and perhaps rare and secondly that I possessed quite a lot of it!"

Rather than consigning his bounty to the loft "to lay unloved for another ten years", he decided to do something with the instruction sheets and turned them into a collection.

What is the appeal of Airfix I asked? "Simply, that during my modelling years the kits most freely available in England were the Airfix range," David said. "FROG didn't seem to be on as many shop shelves, Tamiya didn't exist and the American kit ranges (Monogram, etc.) were simply too scarce, too big and too expensive for a small boy. So my box of instruction sheets were 80 per cent Airfix. I had mostly Airfix, I had made mostly Airfix and through making the models, I felt I 'knew' Airfix."

Before embarking on a part-time career as an authority on Airfix, David had to be sure he knew enough about the firm. "You can't start collecting antique furniture just because you have one old bookshelf in the living room. I sensed also that Airfix kits were collectors' items, having seen some old plastic bag models on sale at what seemed very unlikely prices. If I was going to collect, and especially buy, I needed to know some more. I started by buying a few old catalogues. Just seeing the pictures of old favourites really got my interest going again, after all those years since making my 'SRN-1' hovercraft and Auster 'Antarctic'. Then I had a bright idea! I'd produce a catalogue! Of course, nobody had done this before, and of course I was the world's expert! Full of enthusiasm for this project I put an entry in an internet newsgroup announcing to hundreds of millions of people that they should soon expect the *Dave James Complete Airfix Kit Catalogue*. And on CD-ROM too!"

AIRFIX-72 SCALE
F-4B PHANTOM II

'F-4B Phantom II', 1971.

David says he "was soon put right". Discovering that he "wasn't an expert", and neither was he "doing something new". He says he was pointed towards my early *Model World of Airfix* and P.A. Lewarne's *Enthusiasts Guide To Airfix Models*, both of which I bought quickly. I can't better these reference works, nor do I now intend to," he added. The cheque's in the post David.

David's favourite Airfix kits are the 'Catalina', 'Evening Star' and 'Freddy Flameout'. His most wanted is Airfix's promotional 'Fireball XL5' model – so that's you and 20,000 others then, David! Most modelers of our generation either built dozens of Airfix 'Spitfires' or 'Messerschmitts'. David built the latter: "Lots of ½nd 'Bf109G-6's in all different colour schemes and markings," he remembered proudly.

His ambition? "To complete my 'Header Card' collection. I have most of the planes, all the AFVs, most of the trackside stuff, but I'm still looking for many of the cars and ½th figures."

Summarising, David says: "I'm content collecting what I can find, buying and selling a little bit to make it

Before they were bought by Humbrol, Airfix had their own paint brand.

more interesting, and generally finding out more and more things about Airfix that were unknown to that small boy making models so many years ago."

Dean Milano was born in Milwaukee in 1951. Since then, he has packed the experiences of a dozen lifetimes into little more than 50 years. Dean is musician, traveller, 'Americas Cup' crewman, Toy & Model Museum proprietor, model car enthusiast (America's *Scale Auto Enthusiast* magazine named him one of the Top 20 'most memorable characters' in the model car hobby) and for a decade, one of Revell-Monogram's Consumer Services and Product Development executives. Phew!

A keen plastic modeller since childhood, in 1965 Dean won his first model contest trophy at a local hobby shop. After graduating from college and with modelling still little more than a hobby, Dean's chosen vocation was music. His first band, the 'Casulaires', were very popular in Illinois and actually cut a single in the Chicago studios which Bob Dylan was to hire some years later. Dean joined the 'New Seekers' as bass player in 1980 and for the next four years he toured all over the USA with them. His career in music and entertainment saw him share the stage with the likes of Bo Diddley,

Chubby Checker, The Spencer Davis Group, Jim Belushi and Joan Rivers. However, by the early 1990s he foresaw the end of his live touring days and returned to the world of models.

When he first joined the recently merged Revell-Monogram, Dean initially worked in an office at the so-called 'Plant II' at Des Plaines but soon moved to their more famous location at Morten Grove, purpose-built for Monogram in 1961.

At Revell-Monogram, Dean is involved with the production progress of new models throughout their entire journey from concept to manufacture. His duties range from researching and writing the descriptive copy on the side of boxes to detailing product codes and skill levels. Much of his time is involved in liaising with the company's graphics department and telling them what information needs to be communicated to the consumer on box tops and instruction leaflets. An important part of this process involves deciding upon the size and format of the actual box, dictated to a large extent by the size

Beautiful replica of a '1931 Bugatti'.

Another American import.

and shape of the moulded frames within. He is involved with pre-production test shots at a very early stage. He also fields consumer calls on Revell-Monogram's free phone number, helping explain construction procedures to modellers who might be experiencing difficulty with their new purchase.

Readers might think Dean would have his fill of model kits; working with one of the world's leading manufacturers all day – they would be forgiven for assuming that he might fill his leisure hours with a very different pursuit. Not a bit of it! After work, he heads for the famous Toy & Model Museum he founded and has now franchised (a Milano museum recently opened in Mexico), busying himself with a thousand jobs there.

"The museum was a dream I'd had for 25 years," said Dean. It was an idea that stemmed from his love of model cars. In fact it was only when the friend who had actually introduced him to car modelling in the first place and always talked about the model car museum he planned to establish passed away without ever realising his ambition, that Dean was prompted to act.

Originally he intended a museum dedicated to model cars only, but after some thought he realised that this might not be attraction enough for wives and youngsters. Being also an enthusiast of old toys and automated storefront window displays, he decided to combine his model car displays with an exhibition dedicated to the history and development of children's toys. He figured that then, fathers could scrutinise Dean's huge collection of vintage roadsters and modern indi-cars whilst mom and the kids were free to marvel at more than 100 years of child's play or peruse the assorted toys available in the museum shop. "This way I could cover all the bases," Dean smiled.

People from both US coasts and the mid-west visit Dean's museum, usually combining it with a planned visit to Chicago. The content has to be seen to be believed. It is kit collectors' heaven, full of everything to do with the history of plastic modelling – not just kits but accessories, catalogues and promotional exhibits aimed at the trade. Not wanting to hurry their visit to the shrine, some visitors book local motel rooms nearby and study Dean's exhibits without a rush. On average, the museum, which is open from 6–9 o'clock each

Dean Milano's wonderful museum.

The inimitable Dean Milano in front of some classic kits in his eponymous Toy and Model Museum.

'Santa Maria',
1957.

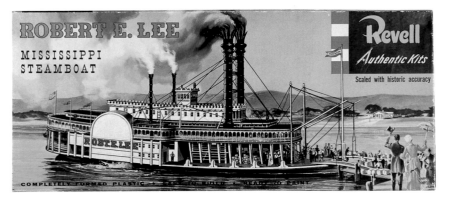

**Robert E. Lee riverboat model
first released in 1956.**

evening and from 11am until 5pm at weekends, attracts around 100 visitors per month. The opening hours are restricted because of the requirements of Dean's full-time job at Revell. How he generates the energy to work in the museum for hours after he has completed a full day's work at Revell-Monogram is beyond me. Together with the 2,000 different kits not on display – "not duplicates" he urged – Dean also has enough spare vintage toys in storage to fill a building half the size of the existing museum over again.

Dean has been a modeller since childhood, when he used to build anything from a variety of manufacturers, as long as it caught his eye. "I didn't build much Airfix though, because until the 1970s they weren't very common here," he said. Together with the hundreds of models on display in the museum, Dean has another 2,000 kits in his personal collection. He bemoans the fact that today models don't have the appeal they did. "Kids don't build model kits any more. They come in to the museum simply to look at the model cars and trucks." Dean's favourite models are still cars, prop-airliners, civilian cabin cruisers and space models – especially rockets. He is also a great fan of HO scale carnival rides.

Dean told me that the US Vintage monster kit enthu-

**HMS Bounty released to
coincide with MGM's
blockbuster movie
starring Marlon Brando,
1956.**

siasts dominate kit collectors' markets. "Just watch e-bay," he said. "On average we have swap meets every three months in this area." The location of Dean's Museum is a stone's throw from a well-established Chicago model shop, so it's an area targeted by enthusiasts. However, he reckoned that although prices for vintage kits weren't rising as fast as they had, because of their increasing scarcity they were unlikely to fall. This is partly down to what Dean calls 'attrition' – the fact that many old kits are built and because some actually fall foul of natural disasters such as house fires or even earthquakes.

Dean is not precious about old kits. He's not a speculator and prefers to see them well assembled and put on display. The supply of vintage models is sometimes reduced because their whereabouts are unrecorded. "There's the guy with a trailer full of old kits in Wyoming who dies and no one knows anything about them."

I was surprised to learn that the kit that started it all for Revell, the 1911 'Maxwell', isn't too difficult to come by and consequently not at all expensive. I guess this is due in part to its massive success and high production numbers. There are many Revell, and Monogram, models that are sought after. Revell's 1950s vintage 'XSL-01

Manned Space Ship' – the two-stage rocket to the moon is certainly one of them. It's apparently the Holy Grail of American kit collectors. Incidentally this space model is rivalled only by another Revell classic, their complex multi-coloured 'Space Station' kit from 1959.

Monogram's gigantic ⅛th scale car kits – 'Big Tub', 'Big Rod' and 'Big Drag' – from the early 1960s are also sought-after models that originated in Chicago. Their series of ¼th scale 'Classic Car Kits' (1934 Duesenberg SJ 'Torpedo Phaeton', Mercedes 1939 '540K Cabriolet' among them) dating from 1963 were produced to the highest standards and are on most car collectors' wish lists. Indeed, so high was the quality of these kits that Monogram were confident enough to promote them in auto enthusiasts' magazines as "being recognised everywhere as the finest car models ever produced".

Dean mentioned numerous classic collectors' items that originated during the heyday of either Revell or Monogram. Famous kits like the 'Autorama Modern Car' gift set from 1956 which included ⅟₃₂nd scale replicas of a Chrysler 'New Yorker', Ford 'Fairlane Sunliner', Buick 'Century' and Continental 'Mk II' – all in one box. The ultra-rare ⅟₂₂nd scale Pan Am 'Super 7 Clipper' Airport Scene complete with boarding ramp, baggage trailer

Revell 'American Firefighters', 1953.

and towing tractor dating from 1955 is "one of the rarest Revell kits in existence and probably built for Pan Am to sell directly to passengers".

Some early examples of Revell-Monogram kits will never be available again, the moulds having been damaged or, far more likely, permanently modified to produce a subsequent mark of the basic car. Monogram's 1969 Dodge 'Dart' is one such example – since its release it has been re-tooled to produce a 1968 'Dart'. So, keep an eye out for the '69!

Model kit firms regularly face the dilemma of irreversibly altering moulds. "It's just business," said Dean. "Making a permanent change to a mould is much more inexpensive than producing a new one. But because that change can't be reversed, the decision is a risky one. You never really know if you've made the right choice and might discover that in future, the unmodified version achieves really high sales. Trends change. You don't know what the fashion might be in 20 years."

Because the quickest that model kit firms can bring a new product to market is about one year, manufacturers have to tread with caution.

Dean pointed out that Revell-Monogram is in business to fulfill a forecastable demand – they are not speculators. Film tie-ins can be unprofitable, especially if the film flops and you factor in the cost and effort involved in securing licences. However, considering America's enduring love affair with the automobile, it's not surprising that re-issuing kits associated with movies such as 'Bullitt' or 'American Graffiti' that prominently feature cars, often bucks the trend and is very profitable.

Fortunately, like all manufacturers, Revell-Monogram have their 'banker' kits that sell and sell. These generally need little or no work to the mould tools, which being made of machine steel are tough as old boots and capable of virtually endless use.

Enough of cars for the moment. Many at Revell-Monogram today are certainly grateful for the sterling

VW 'Street Machine'.

An American classic.

business generated year in and year out by two ⅟₄₈th scale aircraft moulds which date to the early 1970s. Their 'B-17 Flying Fortress' and 'P-51 Mustang' kits have the same appeal today with countless American boys as they did over a quarter of a century ago.

Our final kit collector, another American and … well, all-round expert about the plastic kit industry, is that walking cornucopia of knowledge the internationally respected John Burns.

John is the founder of the 'Kit Collectors Clearinghouse' (KCC) and publishes a series of *Collectors Value Guides* for scale model plastic kits. I have the sixth edition of his guide and recently he kindly sent me his mammoth 'PAK-20' – a comprehensive guide to literally every plastic aircraft kit manufactured in the 20th century.

The KCC also publishes a monthly bulletin, which serves as a forum for kit collectors and model enthusiasts everywhere and is a mechanism for those searching for a particular kit to advertise their requirement.

"I celebrated my seventh birthday on December 7, 1941, but my modelling urges were already growing

'Saturn 1 B', 1971.

'Mercury' and 'Gemini' capsules, 1964.

John W. Burns: Font of knowledge and founder of the Kit Collector's Clearinghouse. Sketch prepared by modeller Eddy Waas after an original drawn some years ago by a Parisian street artist.

½nd scale 'Spitfire', 1963.

fast," John told me. "My first kit was the wooden Strombecker Northrop 'P-61', which survived hundreds of play-time deaths before I was bold and old enough to play with firecrackers! Lots of Monogram Speedee-bilt kits went down in flames as they were launched from the roof of our back porch! Then, I discovered girls and my simple, uncomplicated life was changed forever!

"After one year in college which was a wasted year in terms of learning and maturing, the North Koreans moved quickly to the negotiating table because the word got out that I was in the US Army Engineers and coming to get them! However, I only got as far as Japan, where I served for over two years in a Topographic unit stationed in Tokyo. We made new maps of the entire Far East to replace the very old ones of the early 1900s."

"I resumed my college career, intending to become an Industrial Engineer but two things changed everything. First, I found the right girl and married her a year later. She has put up with me for more than 46 years thus far. Second, I encountered God and His plan for my life

which was not my plan at all. I wisely chose His way and have been a minister of the gospel ever since.

"I retired from full-time service at the end of 1996. Six months later, the Child Bride said, with toe a-tapping and hand on hip, 'get out of this house and get a day job!' And so, 'She, who must be obeyed' had spoken and like my good TV friend, 'Rumpole of the Bailey', I did what she said. I now am the part-time pastor of a small Baptist church about six miles from my house but the big 70 is rapidly approaching, so who knows what will come next."

Most enthusiasts know that John is a man of the cloth but are unaware of the details; I think the previous words are enlightening. But, as John said "Back to the plastic parts of my life."

"In 1971, we were shopping in a nearby mall and I wandered into a hobby shop, got to talking with the owner and said, 'I used to build and blow up models when I was a kid.' He replied, 'big kids still do that.'

"He told me about a group of guys who were meeting that night. I went, got hooked on IPMS (USA) and plastic kits have been a major recreational part of my

SUPERMARINE SPITFIRE
1/72 SCALE
Revell

SPITFIRE Mk II

life ever since.

"My first interest was in machines of the Korean War (WWII was my childhood war, but the Korean War was my personal war) but they were 'thin on the ground' (obviously, I have been to the Mother Country several times!) so I had to search for them. That search, obviously, took me into foreign territory again, kit collecting, and I've been wandering in that jungle ever since.

"I also built kits into models and even won a few awards locally, regionally and twice at IPMS (USA) annual conventions (Dallas, TX and Phoenix, AZ) but my heart and hands were not destined to produce masterpieces of modeling art. I discovered that I had more fun researching and reporting on old kits than I did building new ones and the Kit Collectors Clearinghouse was born."

John told me that after a while the KCC was not enough to keep him occupied, so he soon began producing books on plastic kits. Three different series have been published: the *In Plastic* series (five books), the *Collectors Value Guide For Scale Model Plastic Kits* series (seven volumes) and now, the *Plastic Aircraft Kits of the 20th Century and Beyond* with its annual updates.

"Of course, much of the fun along this way has been

the folk I've met and admired," mused John. "What a different and delightful bunch we are and there seems to be no end to it all. KCC has reached out to men, women, boys and girls all over the world. There are now or have been KCC'ers in these countries: Canada, Mexico, Netherlands Antilles, Argentina, Brazil, Colombia, England, Scotland, Wales, Australia, New Zealand, Austria, France, The Netherlands, Slovakia, South Africa, Belgium, Norway, Switzerland, Sweden, Denmark, Italy, Greece, Czech Republic, Czechoslovakia, Poland, Russia, Japan, Germany, West Germany, East Germany and a few others I'm sure I have forgotten. Plastic has brought us together and courtesy and common interests are keeping us together.

"My goodness, this thing could go on and on!" John exclaimed. I'm sure many who know him, sincerely hope it does!

Veteran 'Jeep'.

MONOGRAM BADGER TU-16

High speed Russian twin jet aircraft
Стратегический Советский Бомбардировщик

Modèle réduit pour assembler

Authentic Scale Model Kit

¹/₁₄₄th scale Soviet 'Badger'.

5. The Future

Well, the hobby has survived for more than 70 years and has entered the 21st Century in pretty good shape. It's true that manufacturers can't expect the volume sales they enjoyed some 30 years ago, but indications suggest that any decline has been reversed.

Commercial stability has partly been achieved by the adoption of more 'mould sharing' than ever before. This enables existing manufacturers to package and market another's original – saving a fortune in pattern-making and tooling costs and often breathing new life into a kit that has been absent for years.

Another factor, which gives encouragement to the kit industry, is the fact that for many youngsters and their parents, building a plastic kit is often a new and creative diversion from television or computer games. Ironically, the hobby often derided as the province of 'anoraks' is a truly interactive hobby. Modelling teaches youngsters hand-to-eye co-ordination and a modicum of history – certainly more valuable than the passive pastime of progressing to the next level of a computer 'shoot-em-up' programme?

HO/OO 'Evening Star' Loco.

Like everything in our crowded multi-channel environment, the world of plastic modelling has now developed niche markets. So, manufacturers either focus on the mass youth market or project lower returns aiming at the serious enthusiast. I suppose the so-called 'garage kit' manufacturers who produced short-run injection-moulded or vacuum-formed replicas really led the way here.

New technology and the emergence of service operations in the Far East means that it is now possible for kit manufacturers to re-release a classic kit from the past without requiring the original pattern or mould tool. All they need is a reasonable unassembled kit and, as if by magic, they can clone the original. Often, when the original mould tool has been lost or damaged beyond repair, this is the only way an old kit can be reborn.

There is no doubt, however, that the traditional medium of polystyrene has been dramatically challenged by the emergence of resin casting. When opened, more and more models are revealed as resin. Not a problem, if you don't mind paring away the often-unsightly excess resin attached to the moulded part as a residue from the pouring gates. And we plastic modellers used to moan about flash …

With such a huge archive of surviving tools in existence – especially those of Airfix, Aurora, Revell and Monogram – it is my guess that the future probably lies in much closer partnership between traditional manufacturers and the new kids on the block who are adept at short run resin. Surely it makes sense for the 'old

FROG English Electric 'Lightning' prototype, the 'P.1'.

FROG ⅟₃₂nd scale 'FW190 A'.

'Dime store' kits from Italy's CCGC.

guard' to join forces with some of the newer companies, releasing past classics complete with additional resin and etched brass components that can be combined to enhance or correct a kit that really needs improving?

My other forecast? I am sure that with the huge advances in moulding and painting technologies, notably abounding in China and Korea, many more manufacturers will release pre-coloured kits finished to the highest standards. These will enable novices to assemble very realistic models without enduring some of the frustrations we older modellers suffered. After all, often it was these early problems that prematurely convinced tyros to abandon the hobby. Revell-Monogram is to be congratulated for showing what can be achieved in this area. Some of their pre-coloured kits are stunning. They are also relatively cheap, which makes them enormously attractive, and

¹⁄₂₄th scale 'Lago-Talbot' Grand Prix racer by Merit.

within the range of youngster's pockets. Anyway, wasn't it the inexpensive lure of 2/- Airfix flights of fancy which took the British plastic kit hobby to new heights 40 years ago?

Surely all the kit industry has to do is provide a range of cheaper items, which are really different and get talked about at school, to encourage the resurgence it has coveted for so long? New, younger modellers are the life-blood of the hobby. Here's to a bright future!

At last, courtesy of 'Mirage Hobby', enthusiasts can assemble a decent ⅟₃₅th scale polystyrene Vickers 'E MkB' tank of pre-WWII vintage.

Two FROG originals which mysteriously re-appeared from behind the 'Iron Curtain' in the late 1980s.

Bibliography

FROG Model Aircraft 1932-1976,
Richard Lines and Leif Hellstrom
New Cavendish Books, 1989

Creating Space, Mat Irvine
Apogee Books, 2002

Collecting Model Car and Truck Kits, Tim Boyd
MBI Publishing, 2001

Aurora Histroy & Price Guide, Bill Bruegman
Cap'n Penny Productions, 1994

Classic Plastic Model Kits, Rick Polizzi
Schroeder Publishing Co, 1996

Remembering Revell Model Kits, Thomas Graham
Schiffer, 2002

Let's Stick Together, Stephen Knight, 1999

Figurines Publicitaires, Jeane-Claude Piffret
Histoire & Collections, 1997

Encyclopaedia of Military Models,
Boileau/Khuong/Young
Airlife, 1988

Plastic Aircraft Kits of the 20th Century (and Beyond),
John W. Burns Kit Collectors Clearinghouse, 2003

Ed 'Big Daddy' Roth. His life, times, cars and art,
Pat Ganahl CarTech, 2003

Master Modeler – Creating the Tamiya style,
Shunsaku Tamiya Kodansha, 2001

The Enthusiasts Guide to Airfix Models,
P.A. Lewarne, 1987

The Model World of Airfix, Arthur Ward
Bellew, 1984

Airfix – Celebrating 50 Years of the Greatest Kits in the World, Arthur Ward
Collins, 1999

Acknowledgements

Special thanks to Ed, Ruan and Ted Sexton for their hospitality when I visited Illinois in 2003. Not forgetting all at Revell-Monogram Inc. who tolerated my intrusion at possibly the worst time (they were in the process of relocating their business from Morten Grove to Northbrook).

I must also single out Mr. Shunsaku Tamiya and the ever-helpful Mr. Yasushi Sano, who promptly supplied me with whatever photographs I desired.

I have tried to acknowledge all those to whom I owe a debt of gratitude. Forgive my ineptitude if I have unwittingly omitted someone!

Bandai: Lynne Roberson (PA to MD Bandai UK) & Tammy Kobayashi. Global Business Dept. Bandai Co., Ltd.

Revell: Edward Sexton Sr. Director of Product Development, Bill Lastovich Product Planning Manager, Thomas Ramdrup Marketing Manager Revell AG, Gerry Humbert Photographic Services Administrator, Jonathan Tinio Graphic Designer, Gary Brown Sr. Engineering Graphics Design Administrator, Kenneth L. Funk Jr. Manager – Molding/Packaging, Angeline L. Pannarale Marketing Administrative Assistant.

Humbrol/Airfix: Trevor Snowden Research & Development Engineer, Michael J. Phillips Export Sales Manager.

Tamiya: Mr. Shunsaku Tamiya President & Chairman, Mr. Nobuo Yoshioka, Mr. Yasushi Sano, Sam Wright.

Marcus Nichols Editor Tamiya Model Magazine, Alan Harman Publisher Tamiya Model Magazine (ADH Publishing).

Ralph Ehrmann

Mat Irvine

Dean Milano

Jeremy Brook – Airfix Collectors' Club

David James

Peter Allen

Brian Knight

Anthony Lawrence – Dorking Models

Paul Emery

Ray Piggott

Malcolm Rolling – Kingkit

Ken Jones

Pat Lewarne – Collectakit

Paul Milam – Milam Models

Paul Regan – President, IPMS (UK)

John Burns – Kit Collectors Clearing House

Tony James – Comet Miniatures

Roy Cross

Claudius Eberl – Gebr. Faller GmbH

The author would also like to thank all those unacknowledged individuals from companies big and small who have been involved in the construction kit industry down the years. I apologise for any omissions and will make every effort to recognise them in future editions.

Index

The majority of illustrations appear on the same or facing page as the text covering the manufacturer or subject and, accordingly, are not indexed separately.   Significant captions and illustrations that are not so closely linked to text pages are included in the index and are shown with the page number references in *italics*.